THE ART OF
CLAUDIO ABOY
VOLUME 2

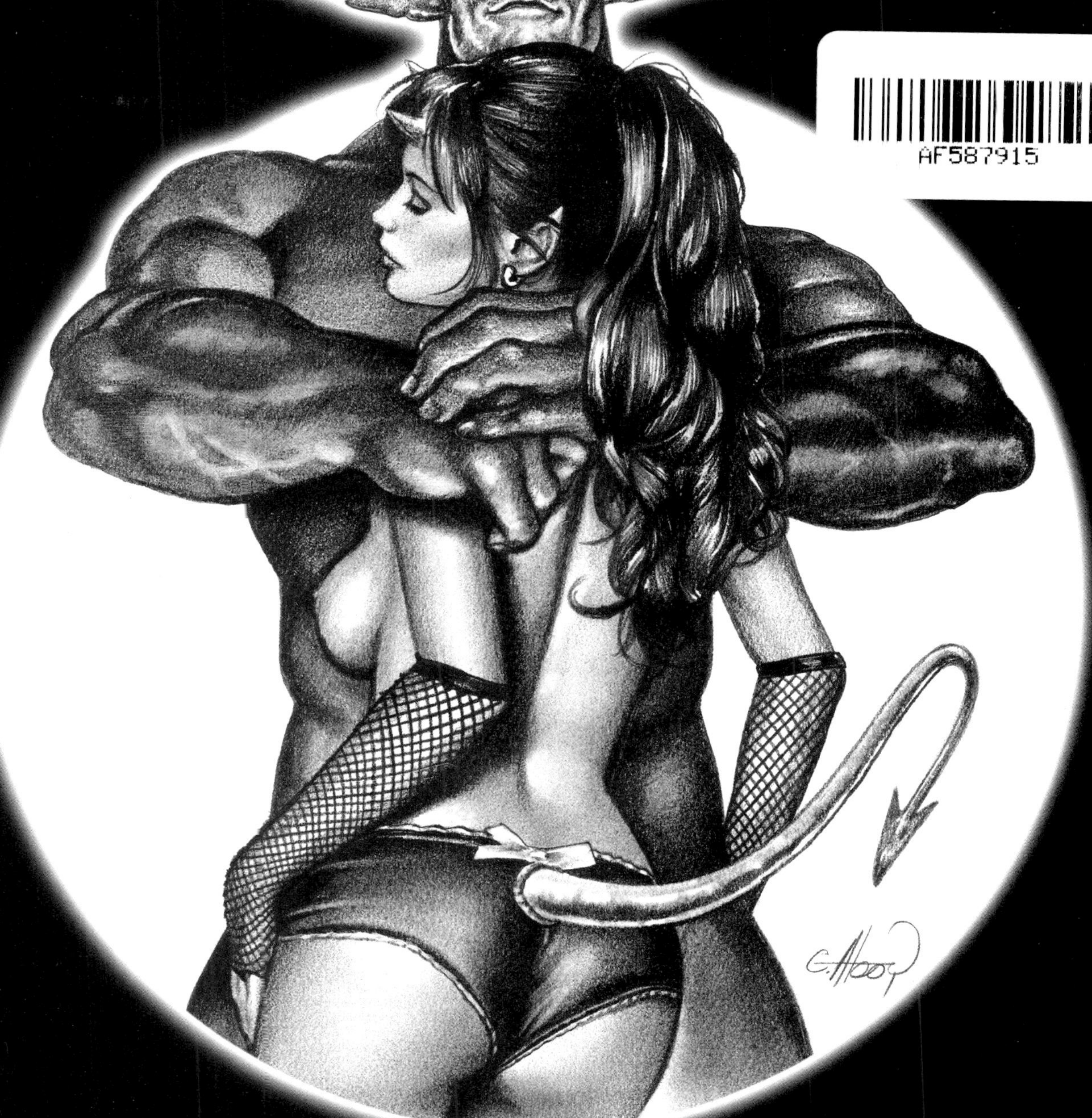

AN SQP PRESENTATION

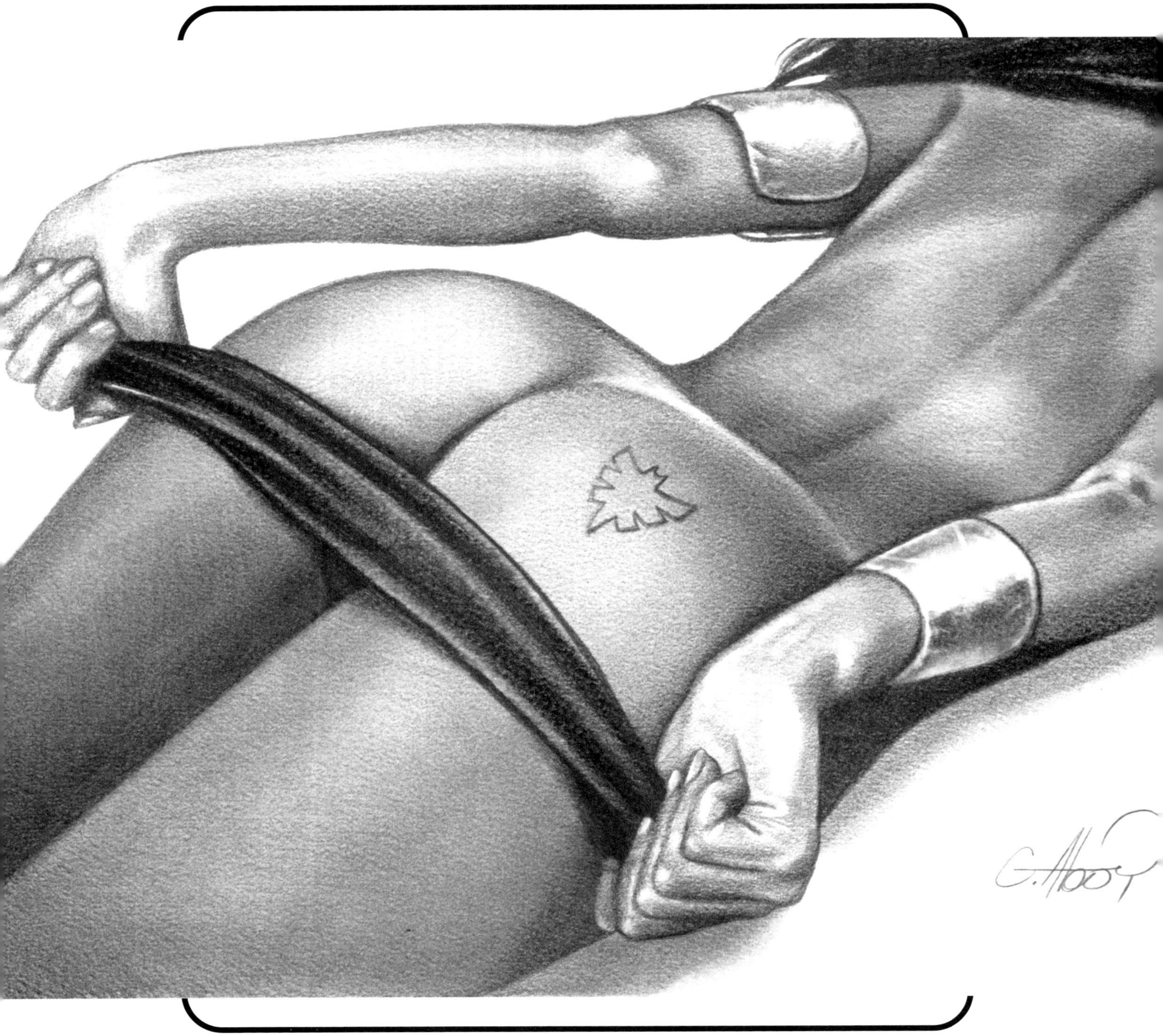

THE ART OF CLAUDIO ABOY

Volume Two

Book design by Grassy Knoll Studios.

Published by
SQP Inc.
PO Box 248 - Columbus, NJ 08022

Sal Quartuccio & Bob Keenan - Publishers

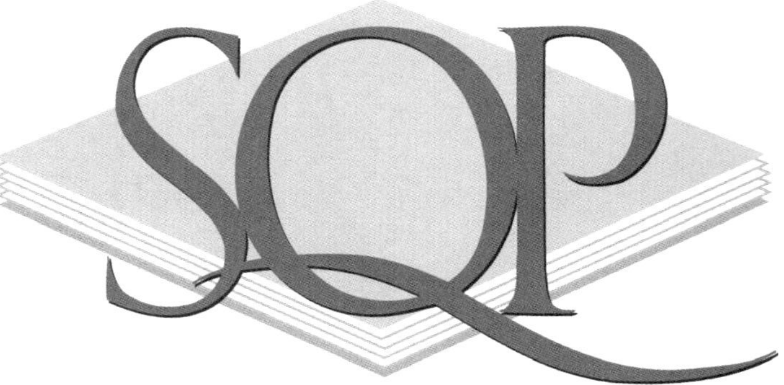

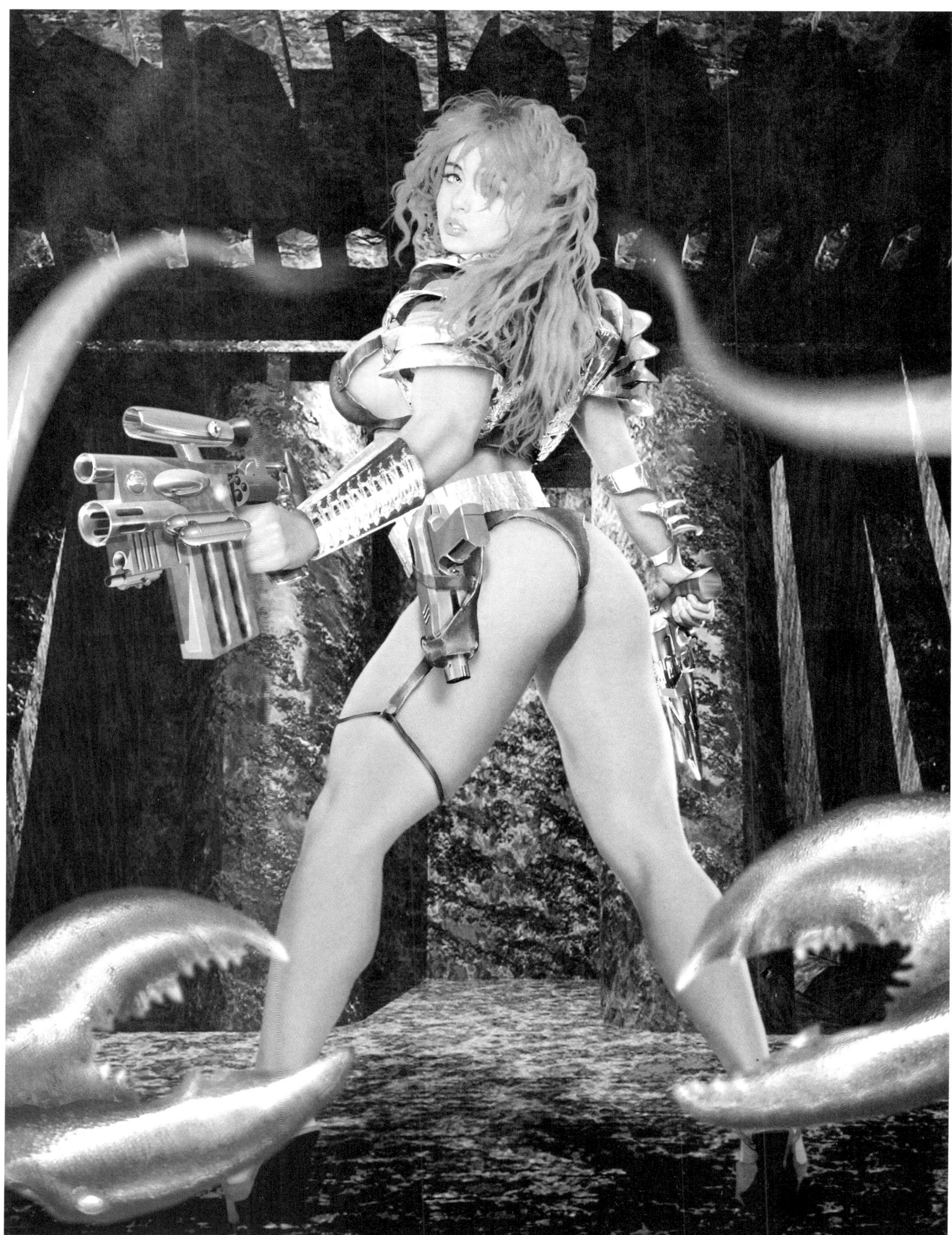

D.O.A - P.O.V.

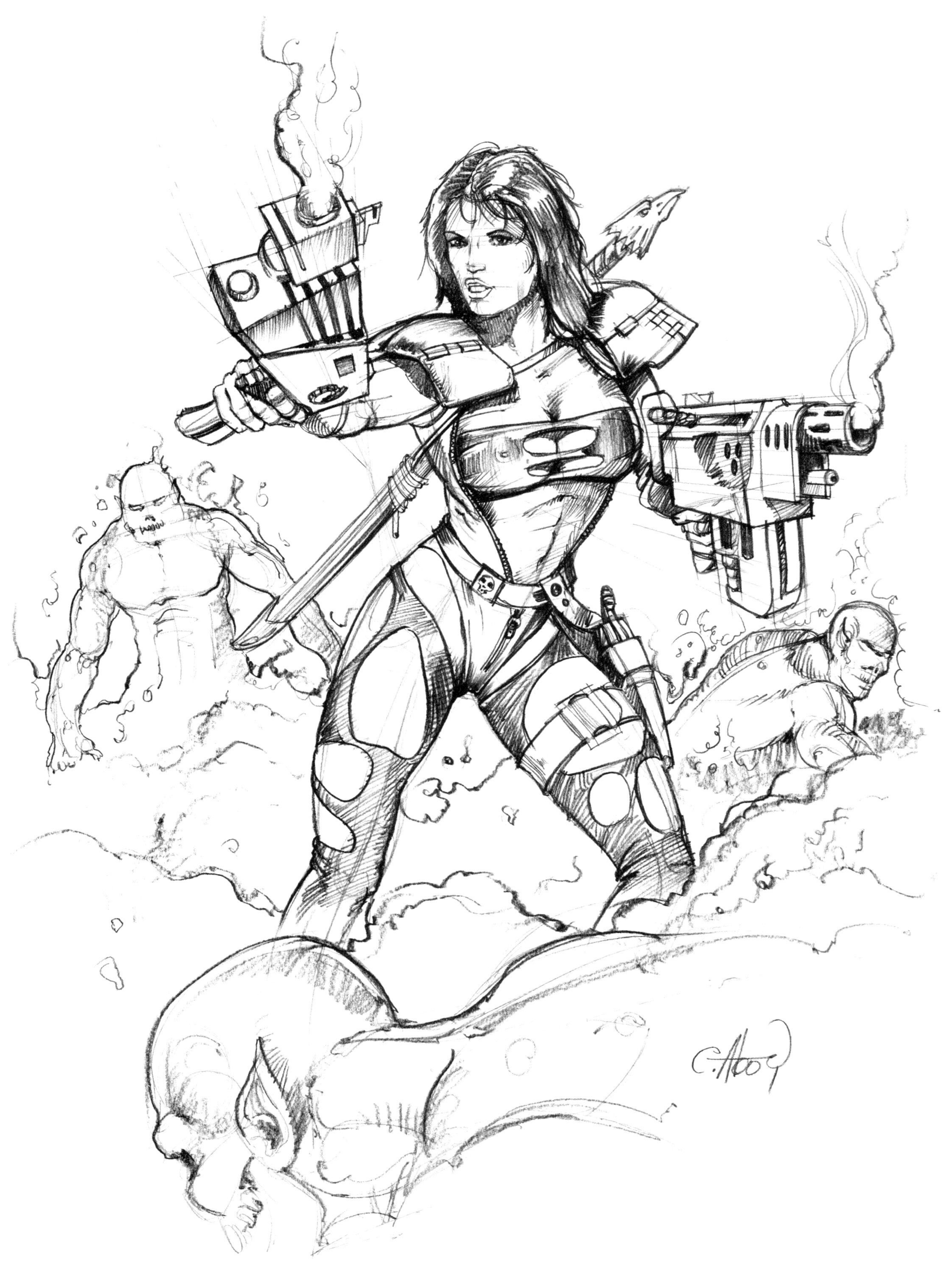

Hell is War

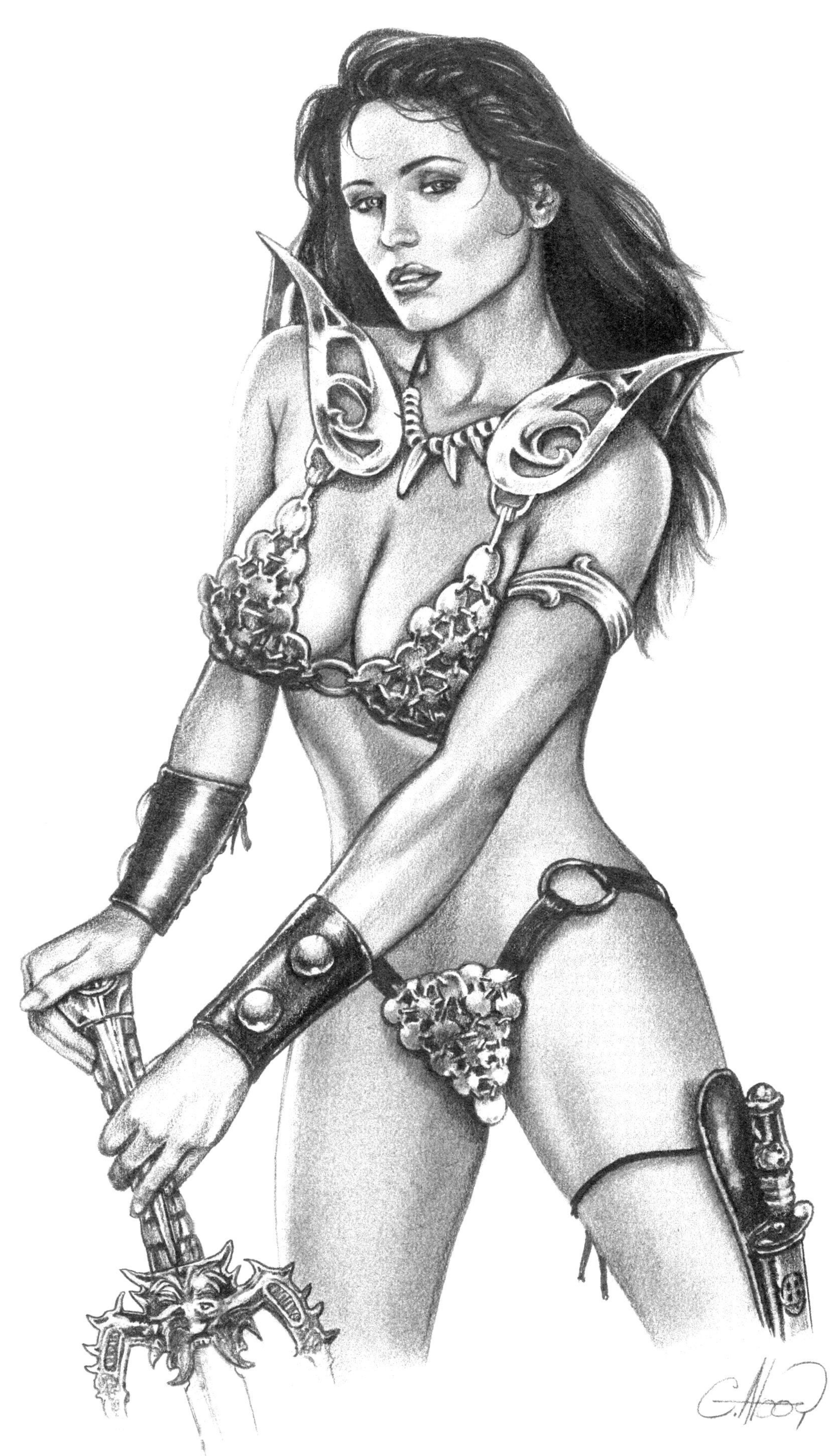

The Challenge Given

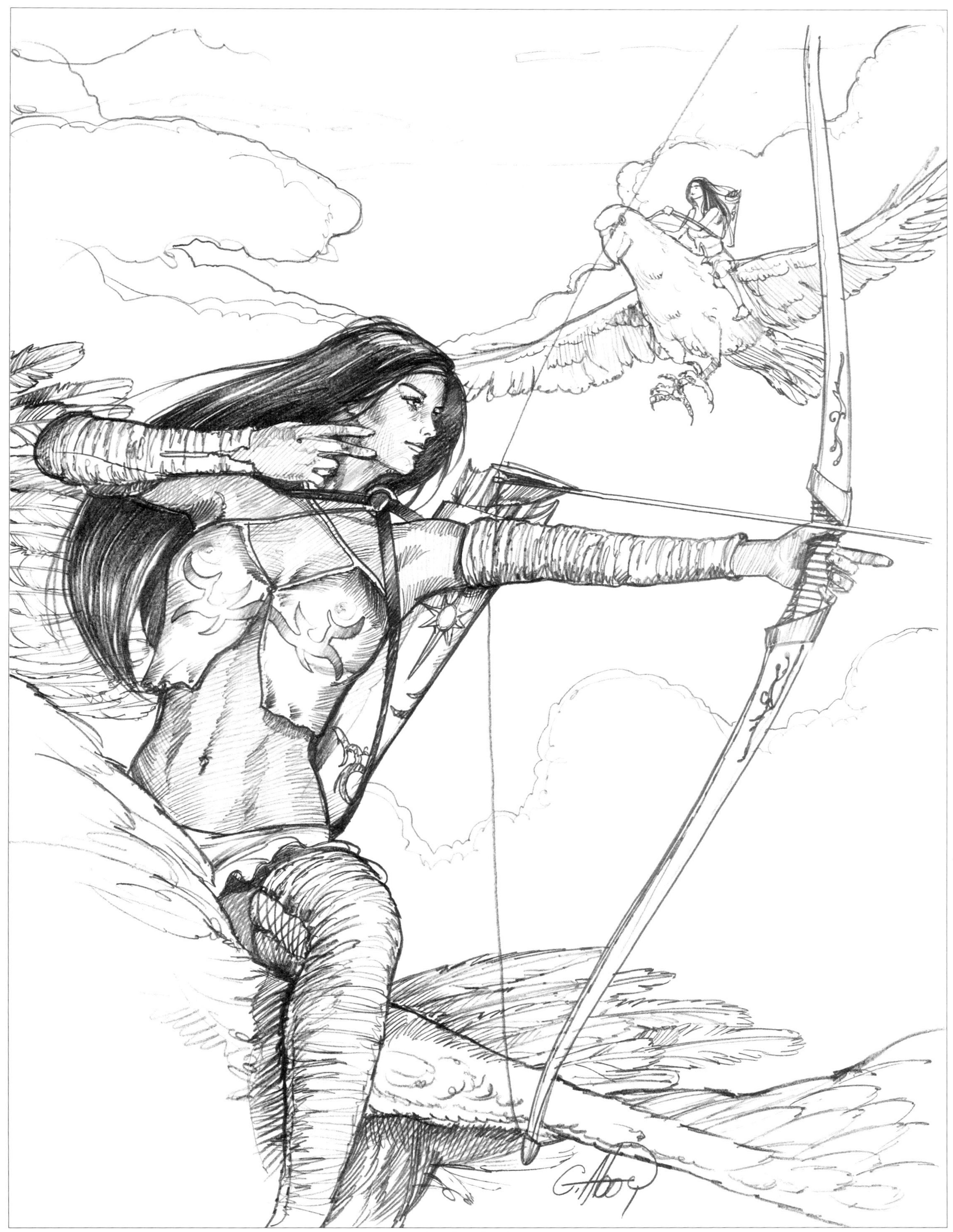

Eagle Hunting

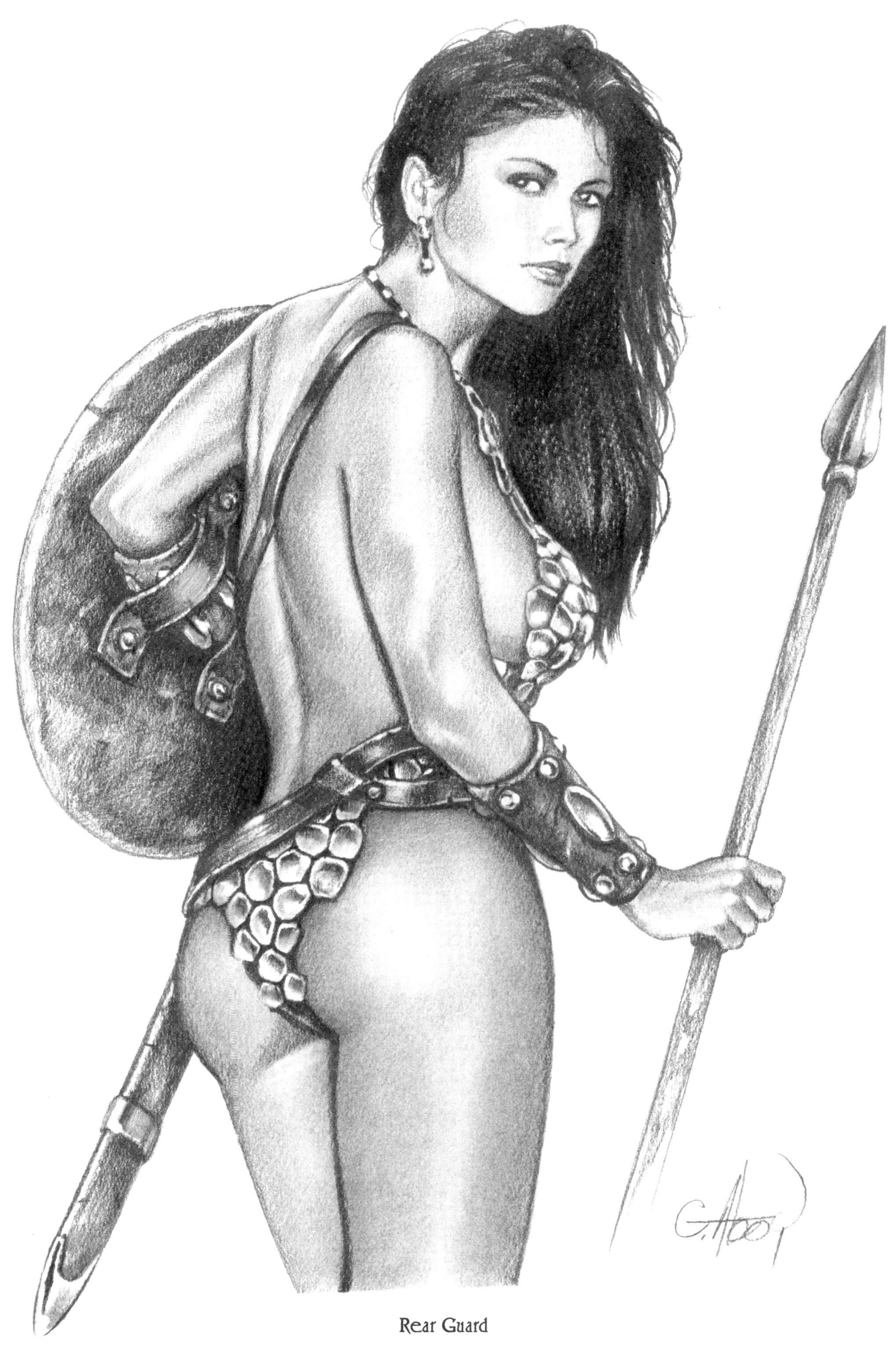

Rear Guard

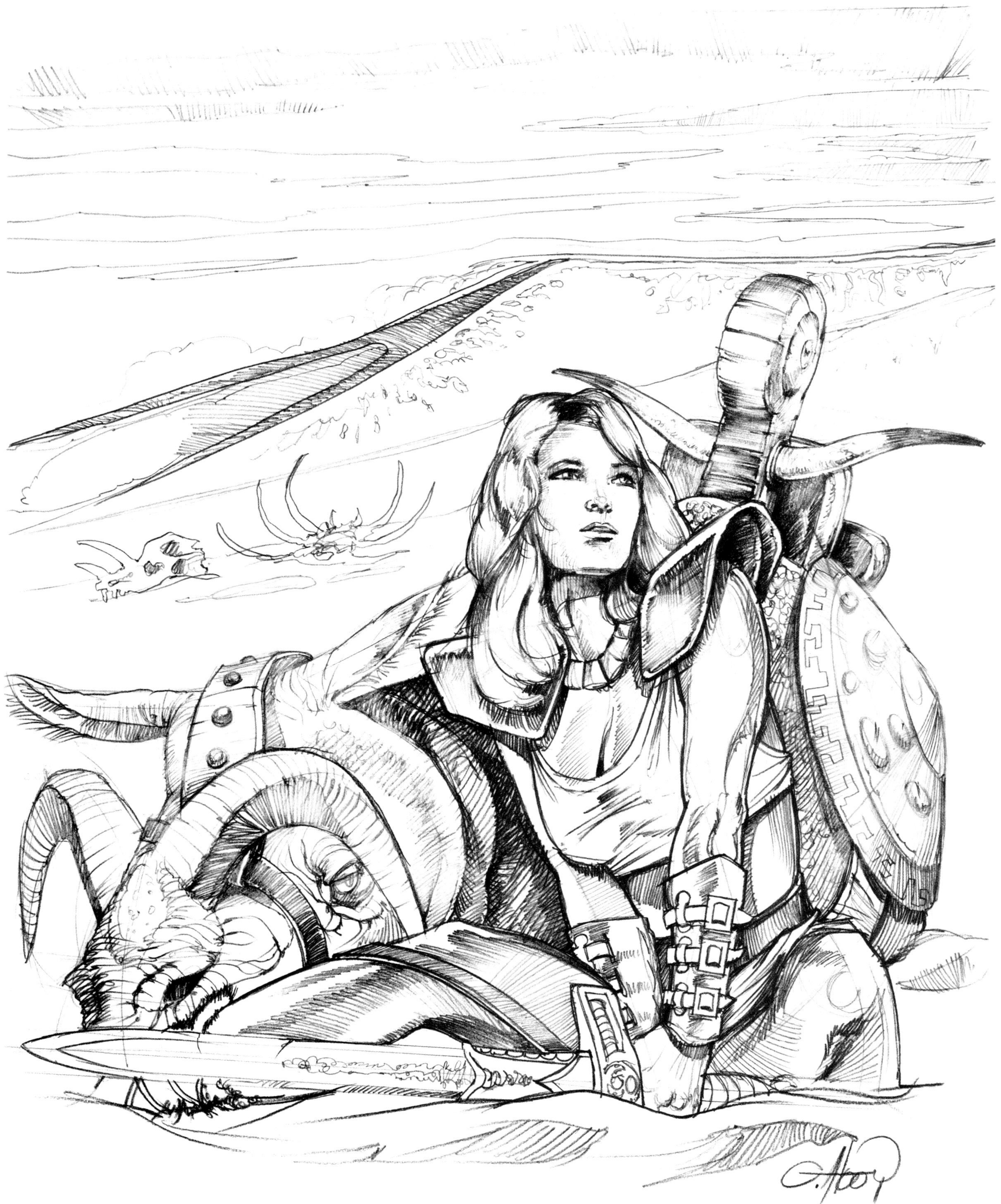
The Last Stand

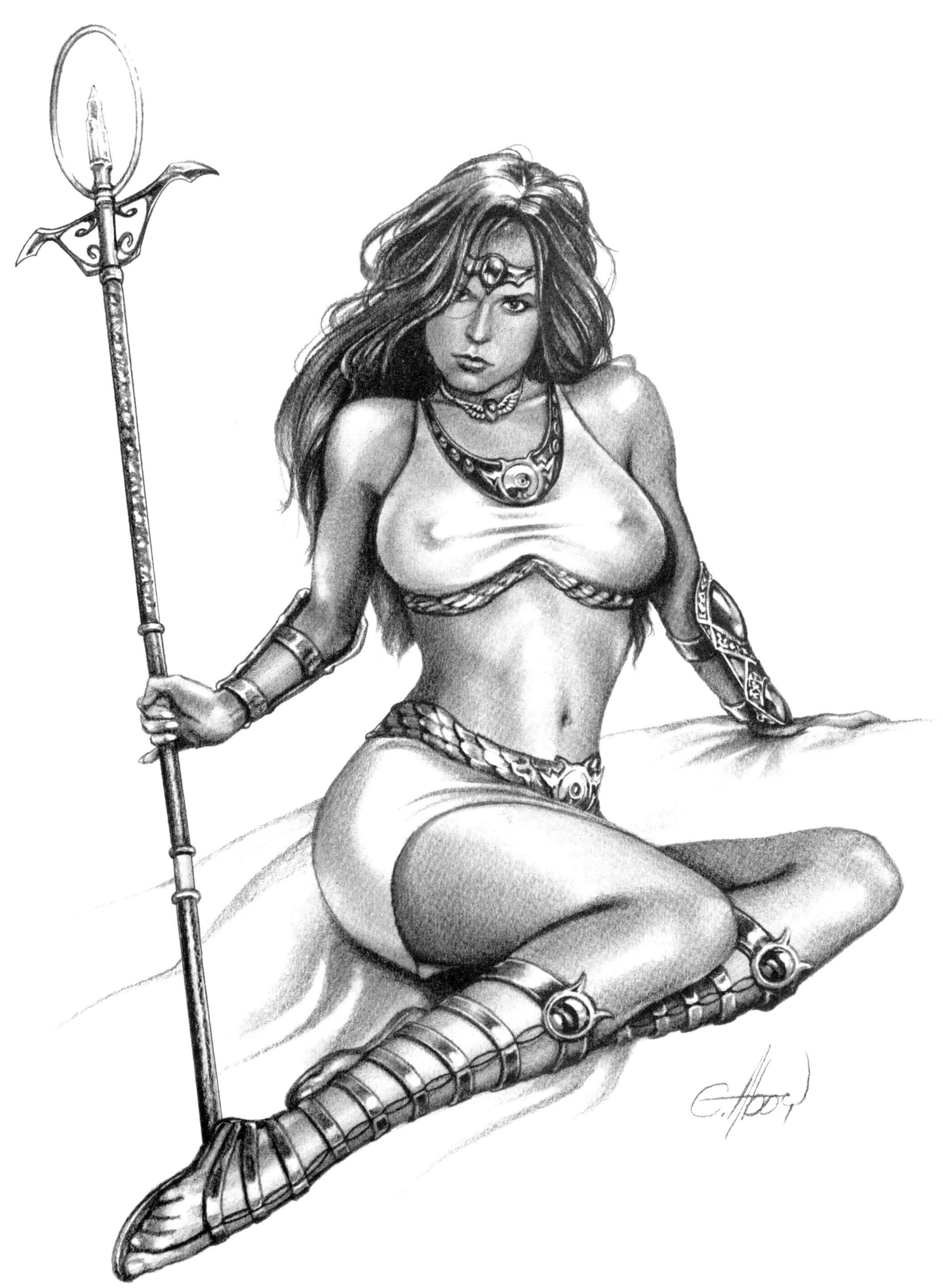

None May Defy the Priestess

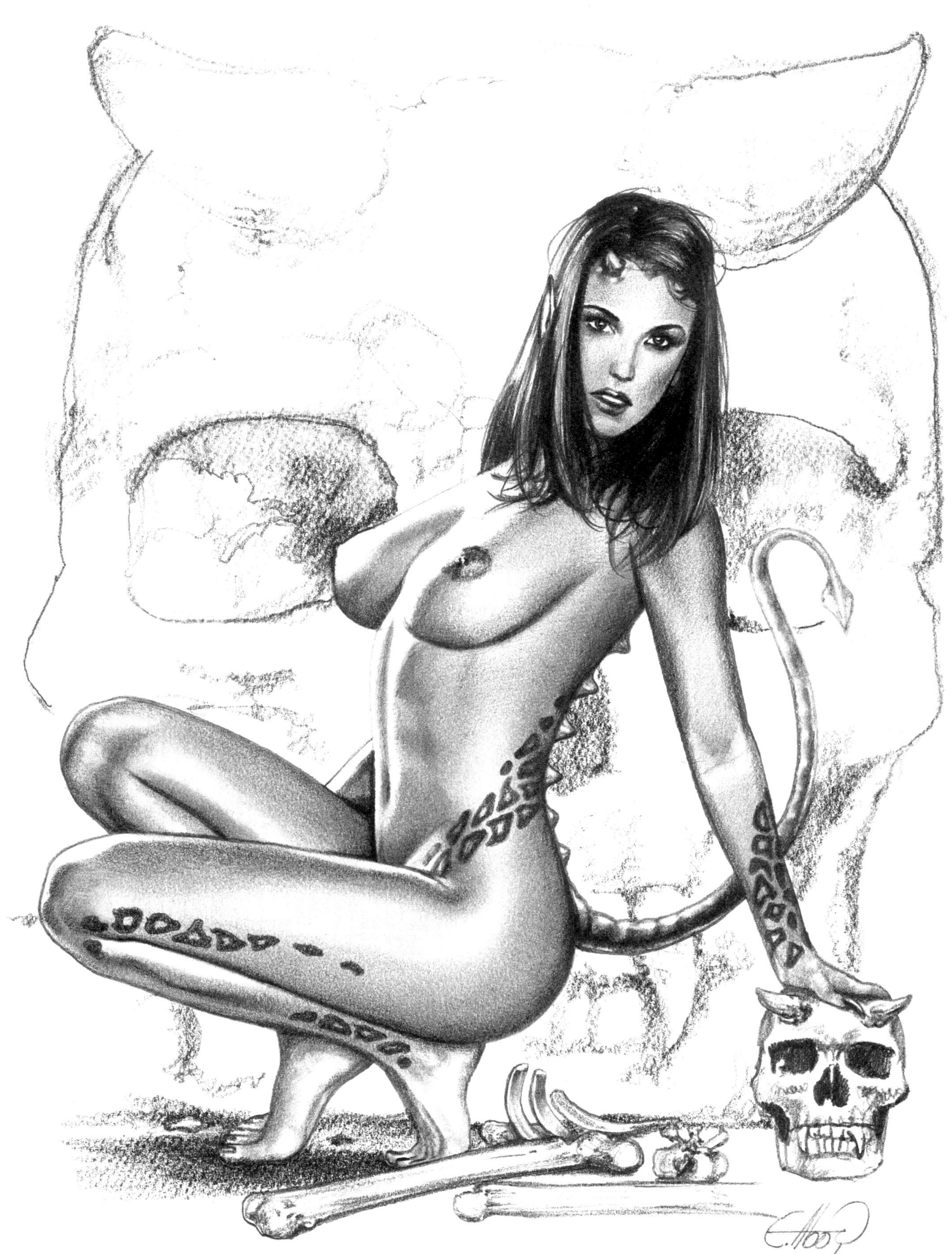

Daughter of Demons

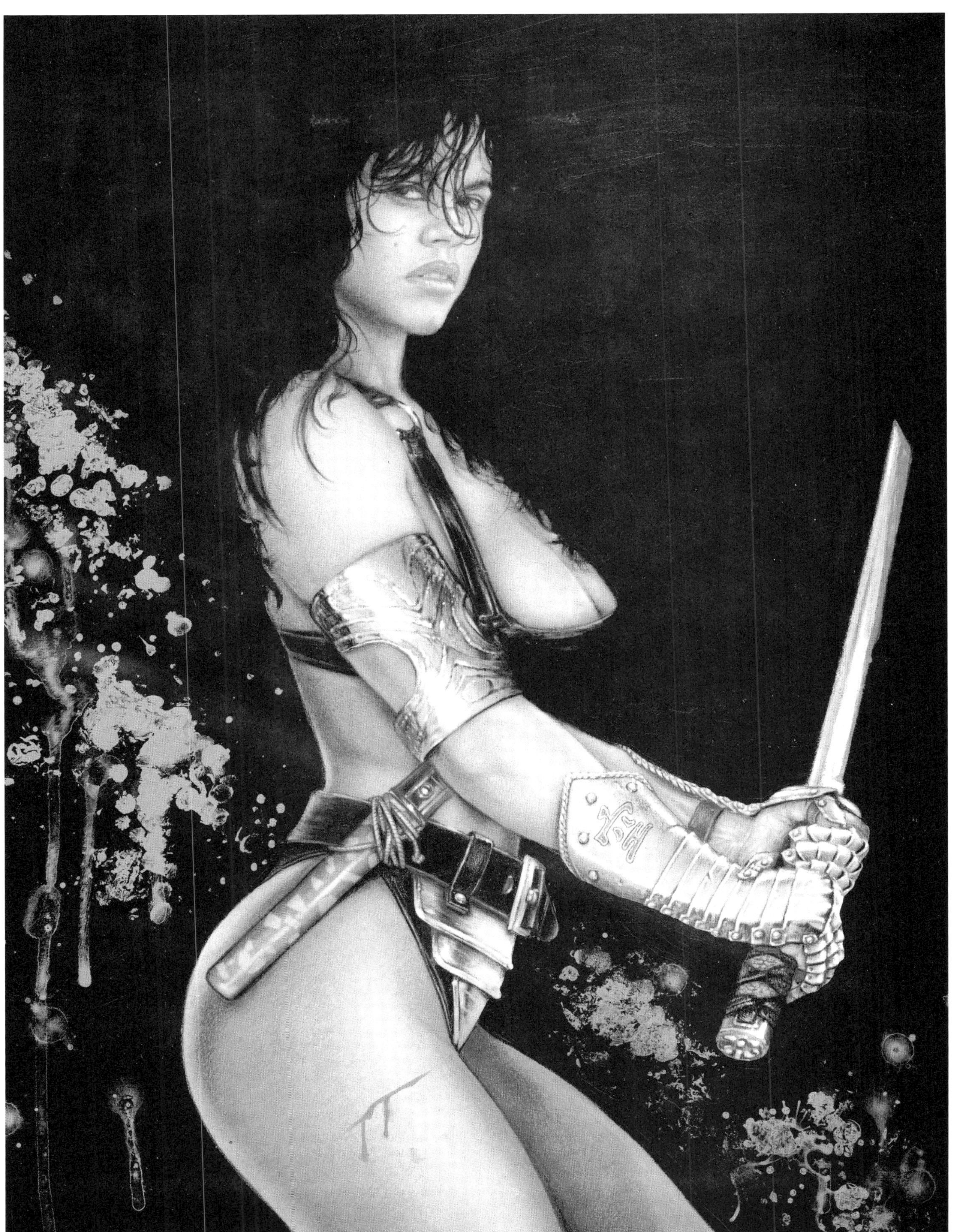

The Killing Stroke

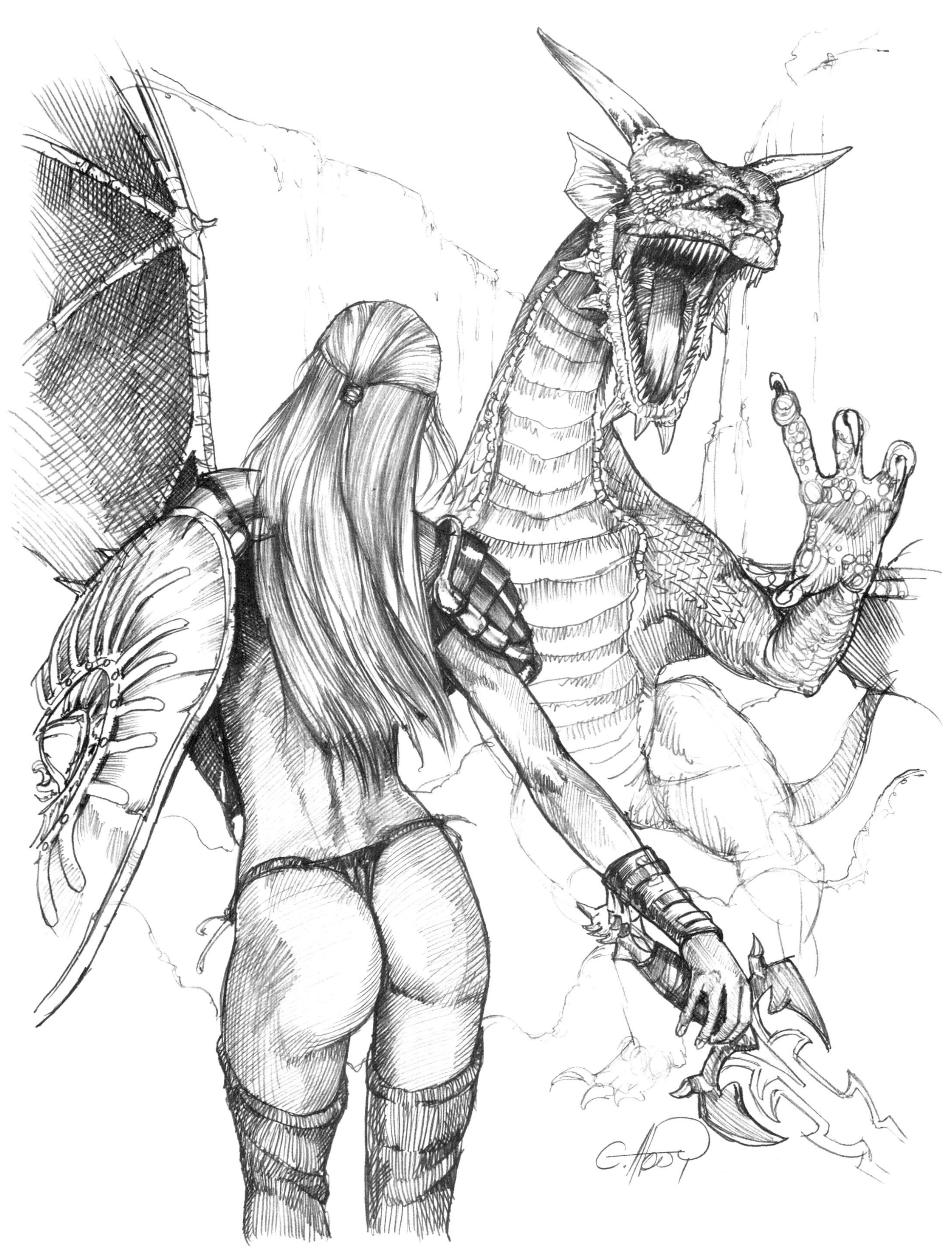

Dragon's Last Day

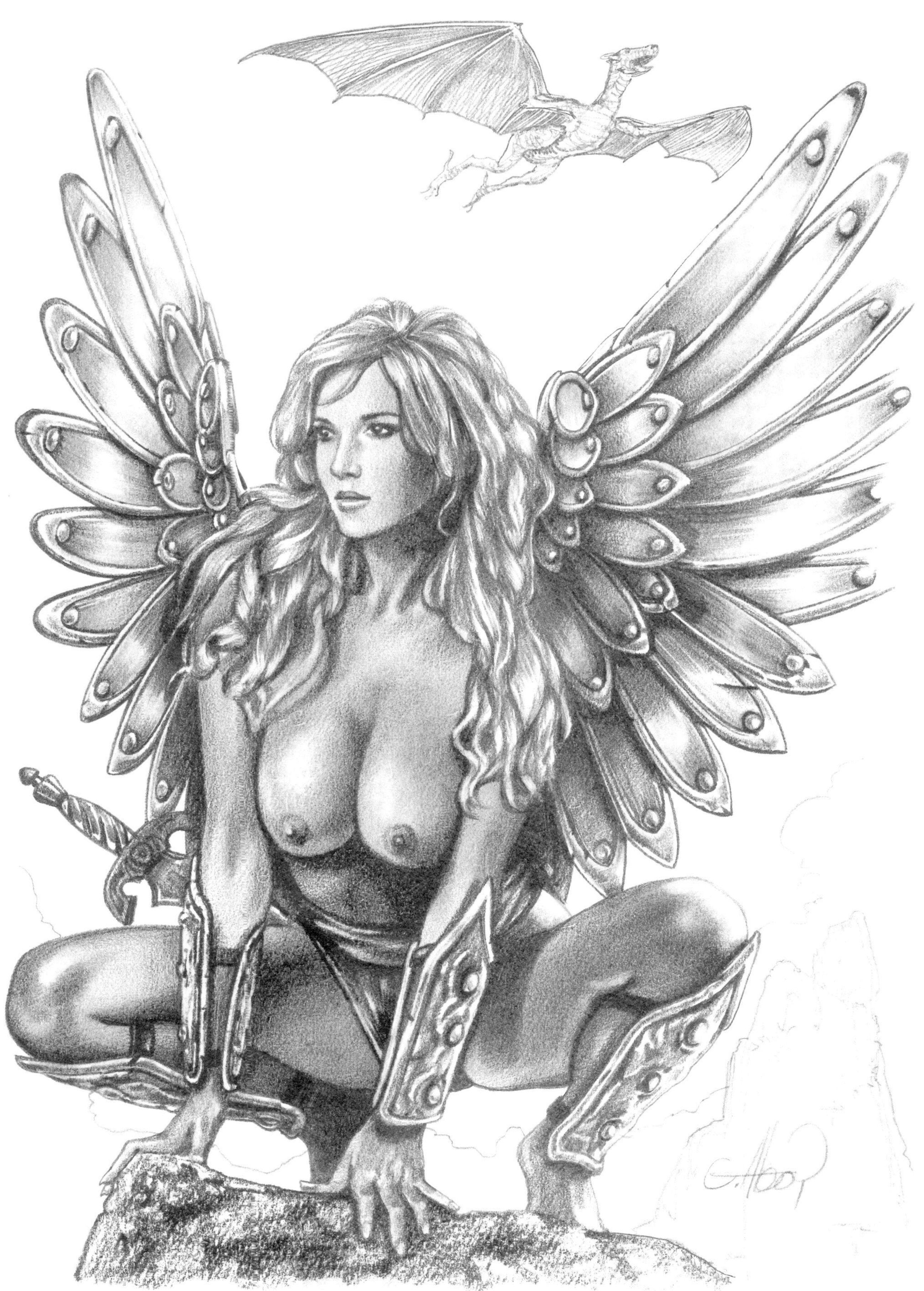

Wings of Gold and Blood

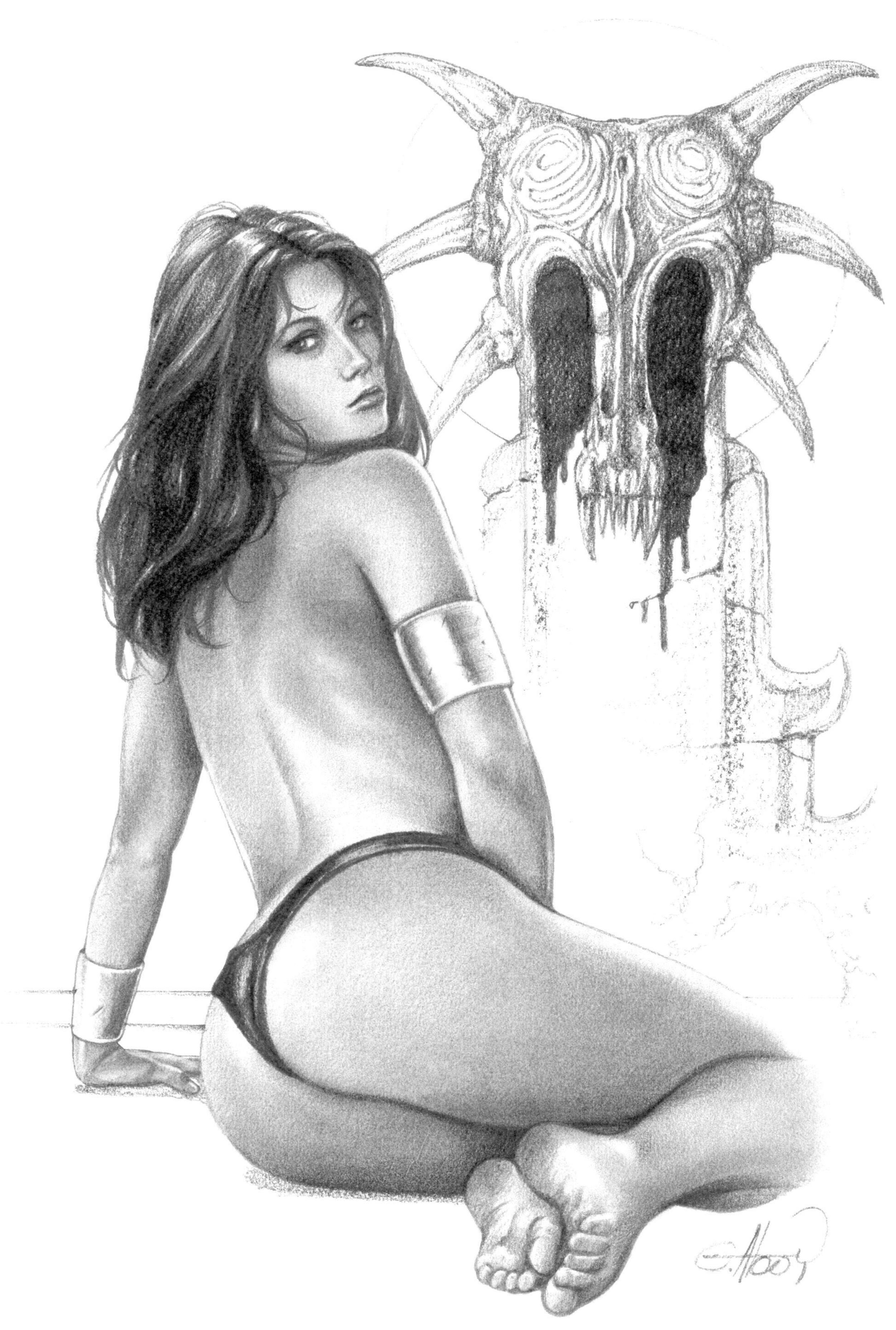

All Glory to the Crimson Gods

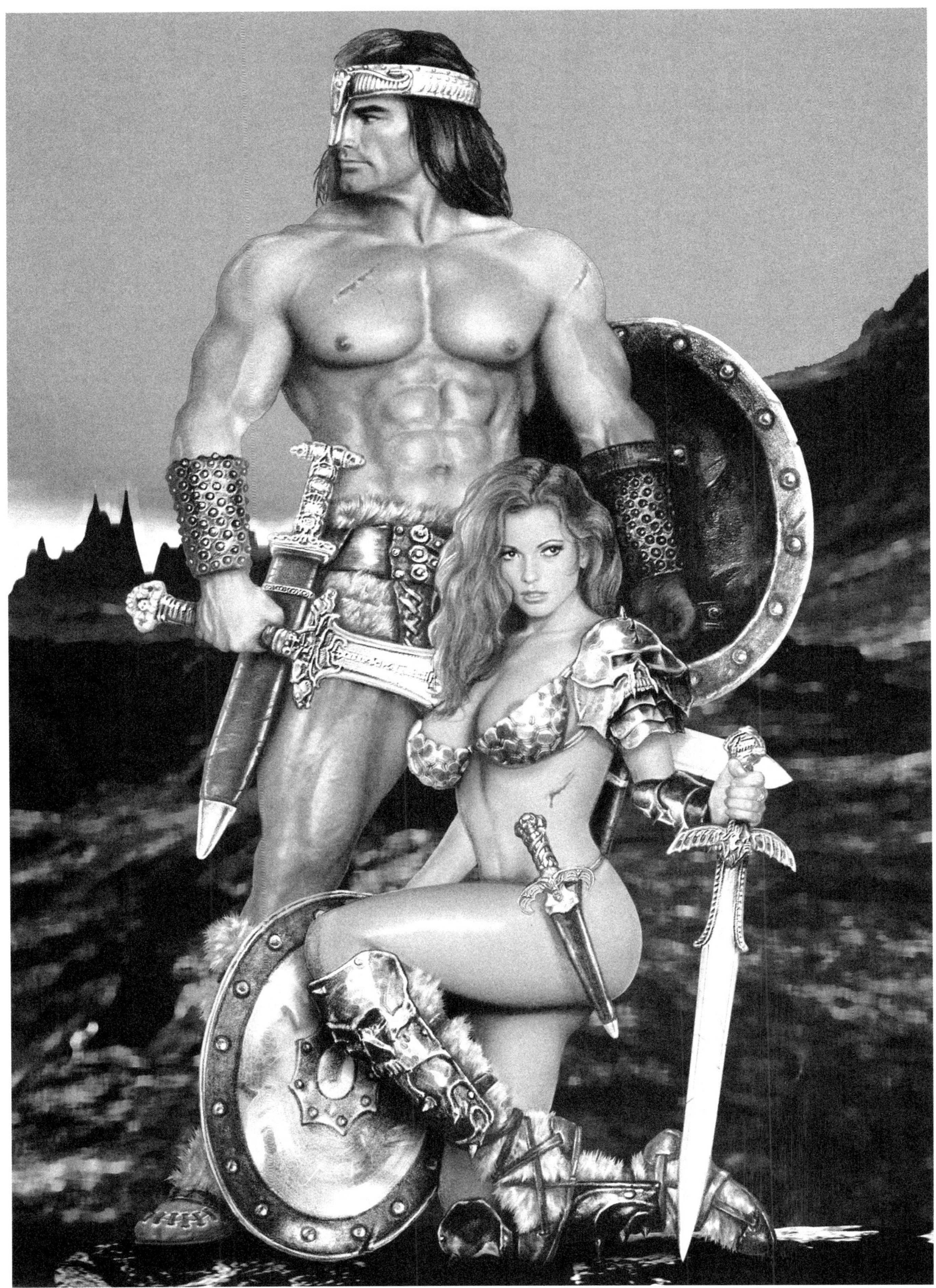

Hearts Forged of Steel

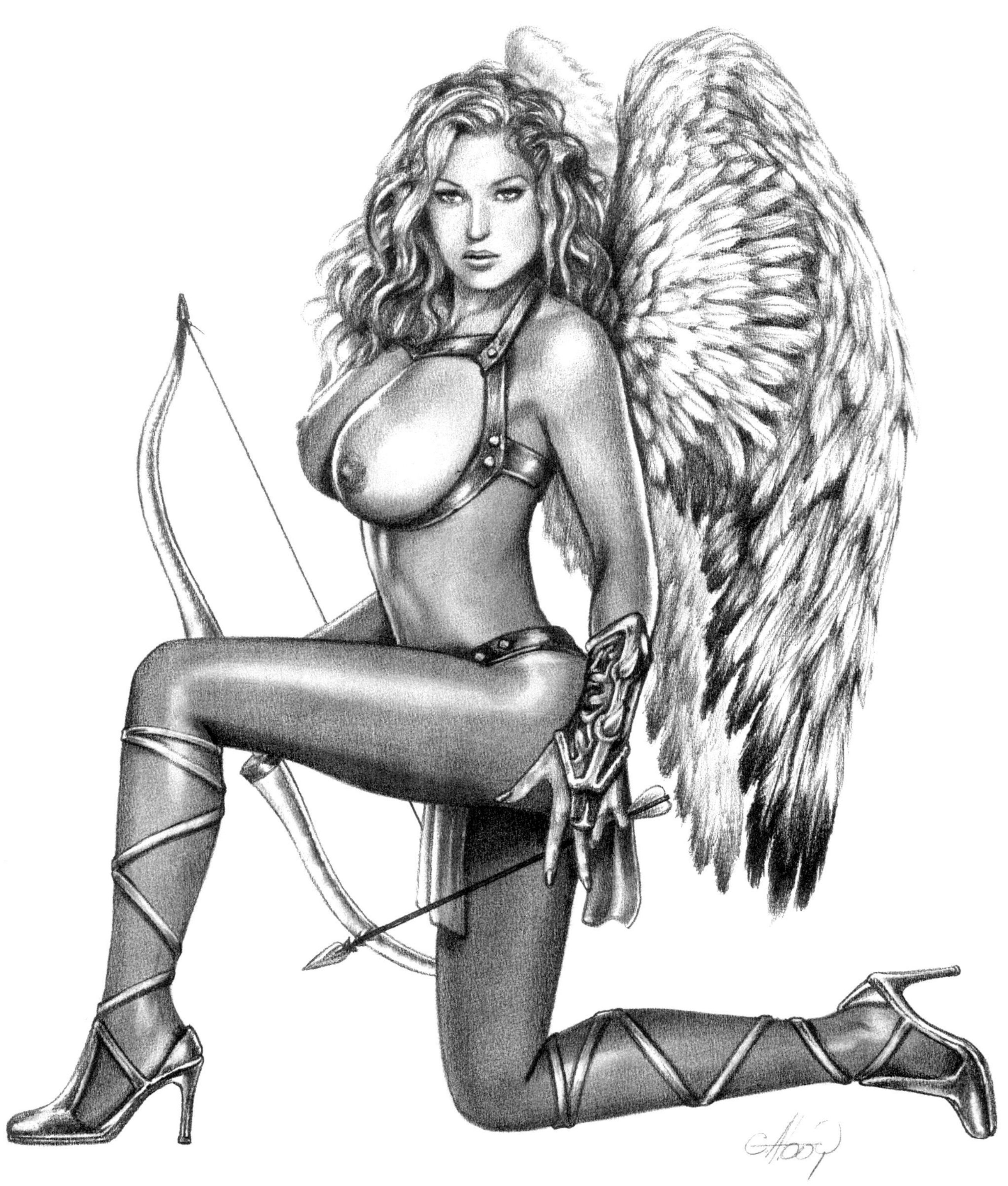

The Fury of Angels

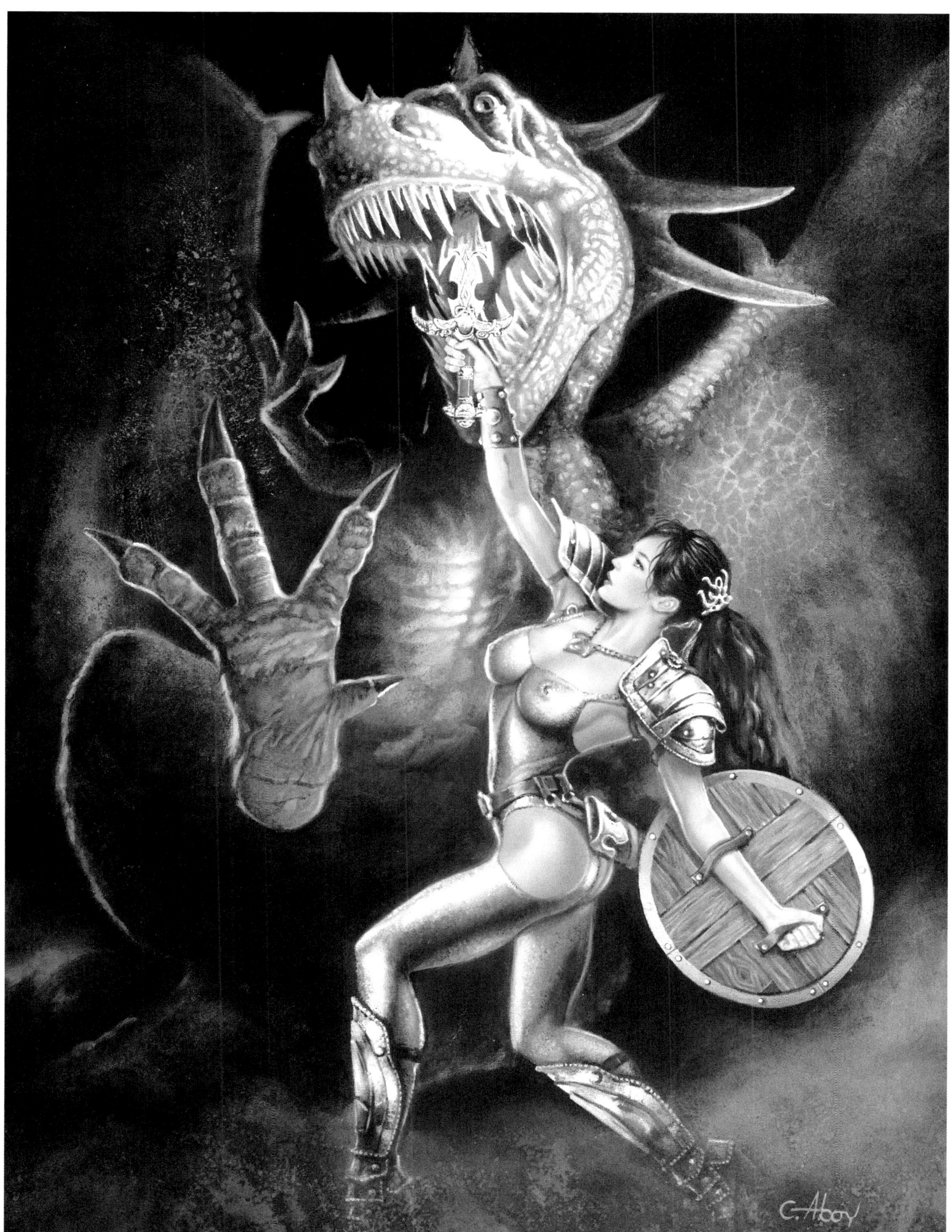

Dragon's Blood

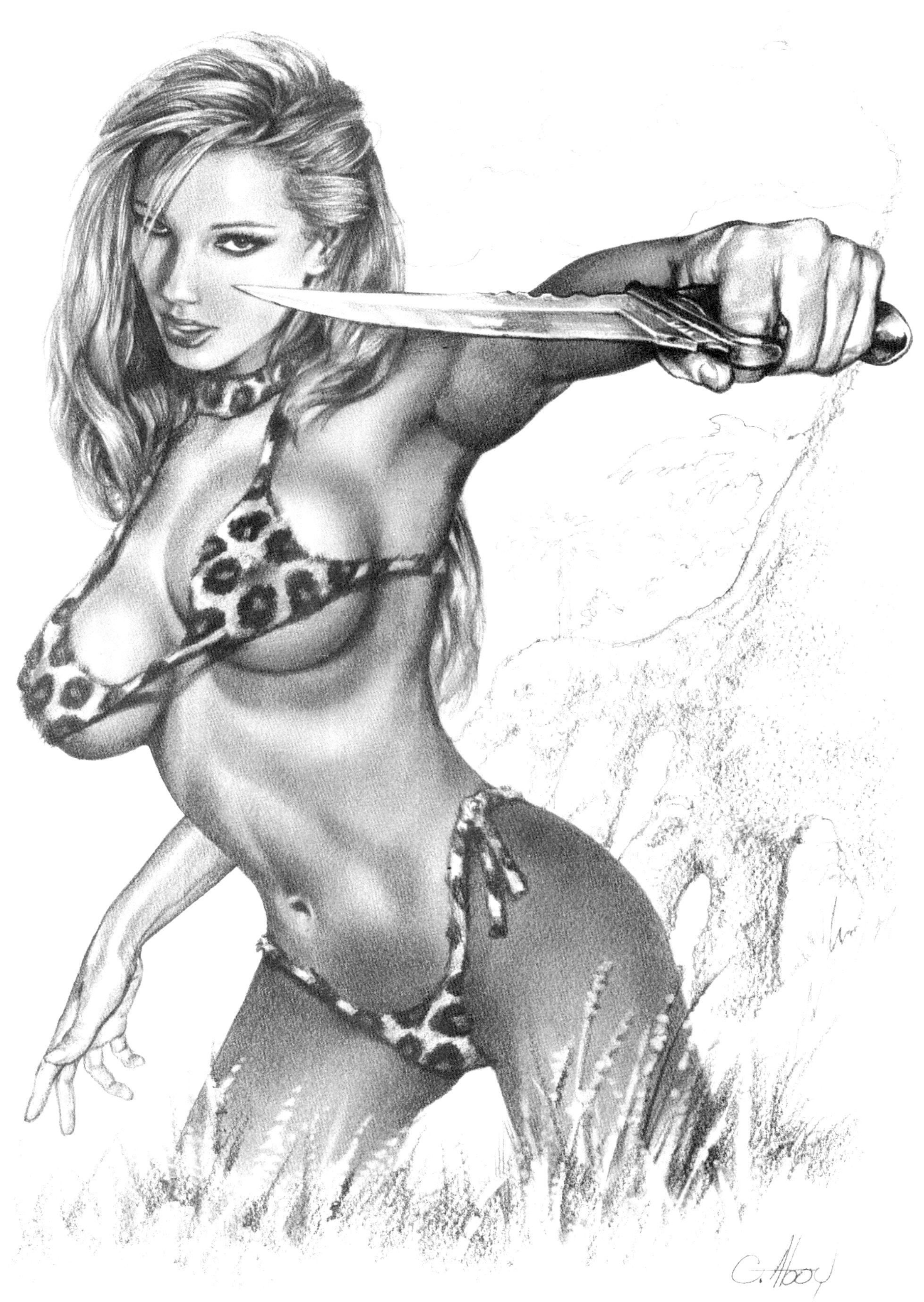

She Rules This Land

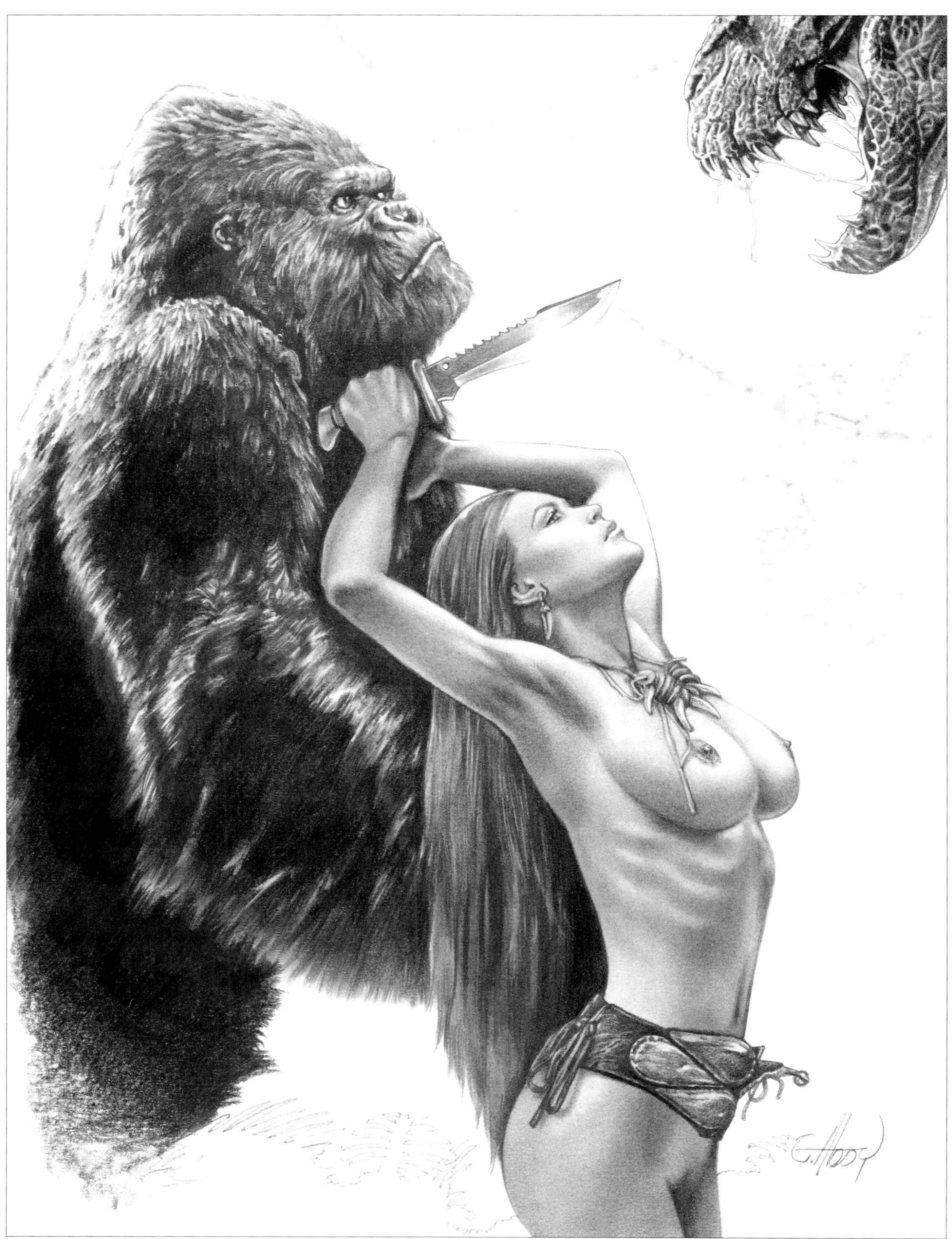

Bringing Back-Up

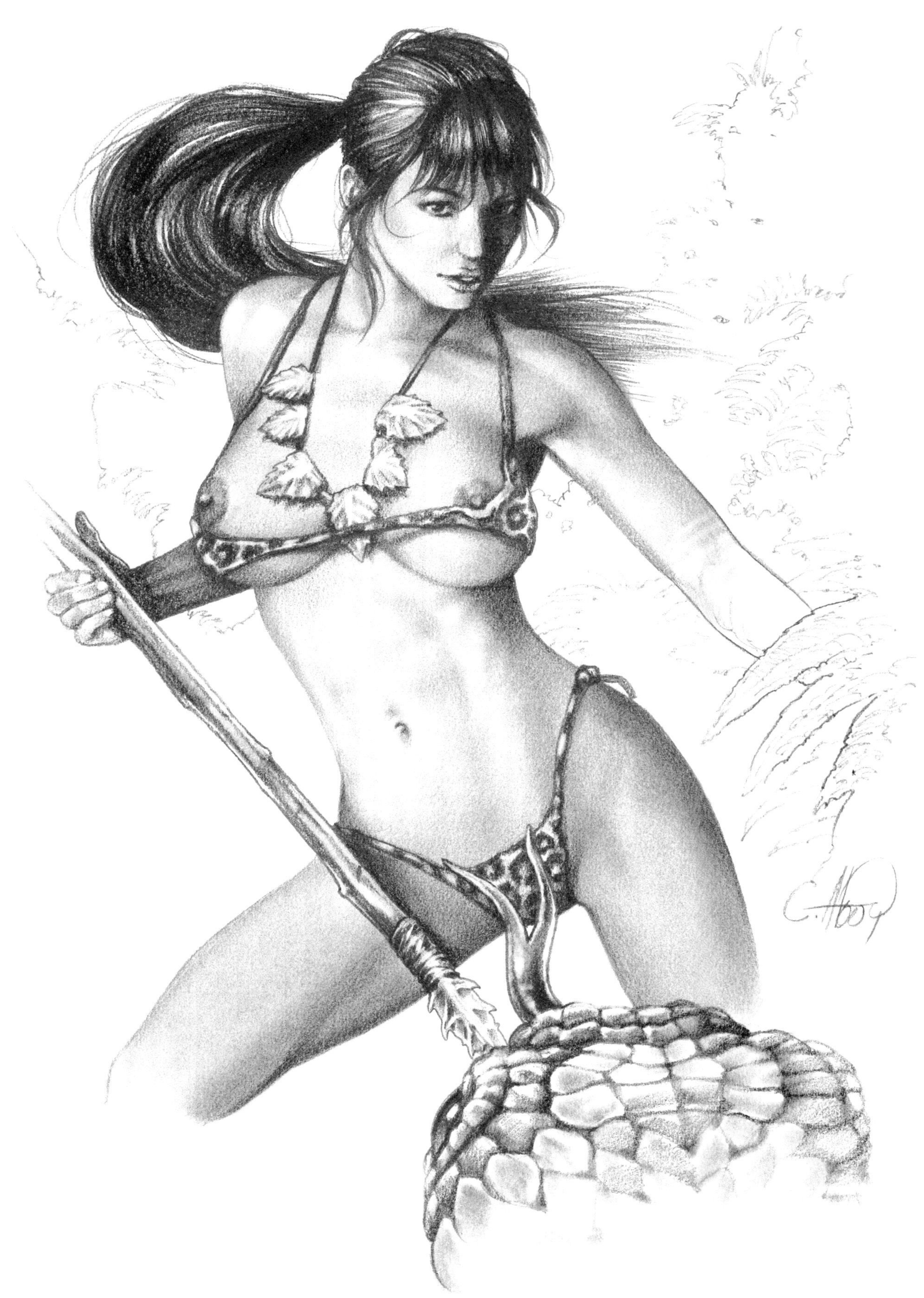

Serpentine

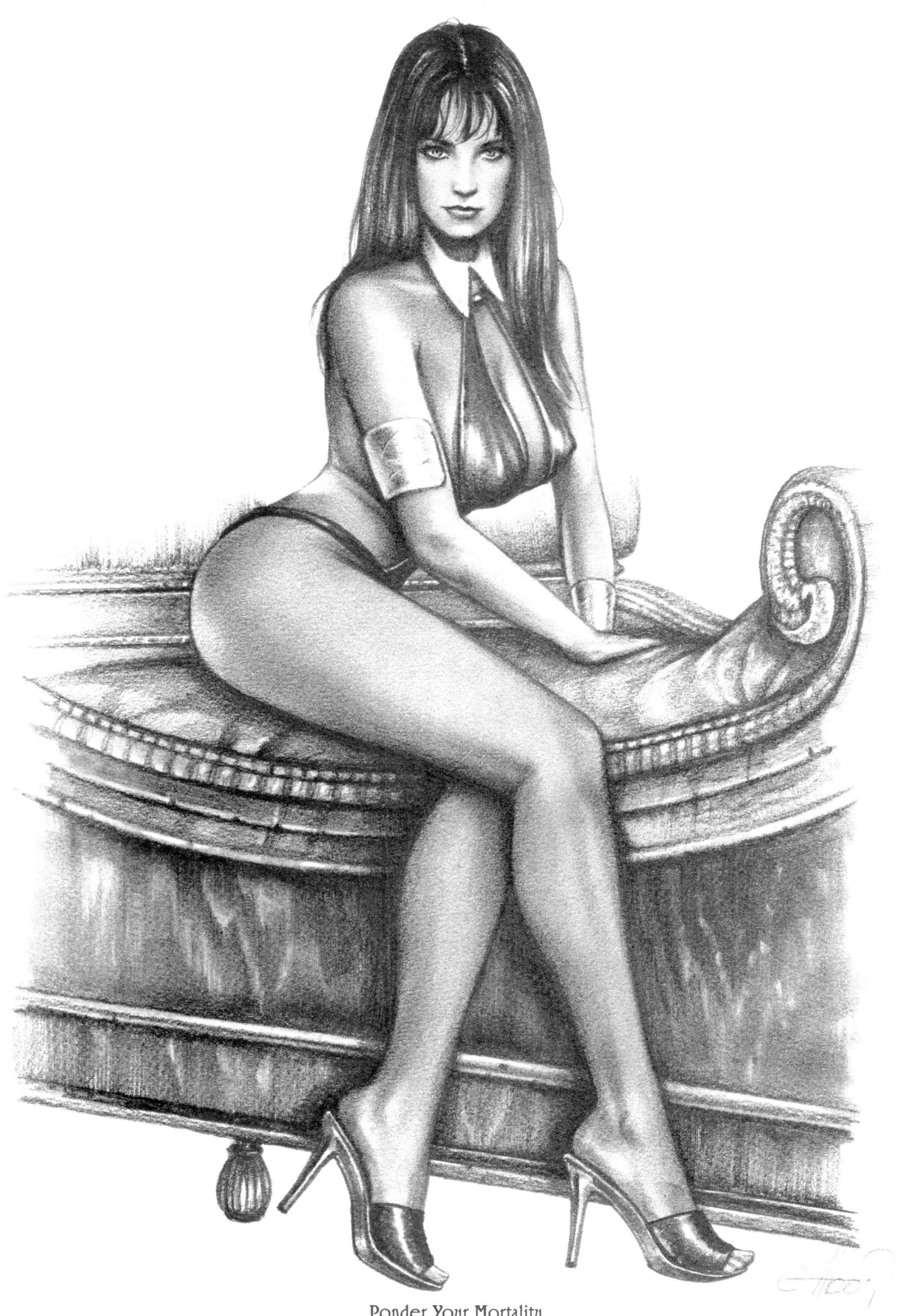

Ponder Your Mortality

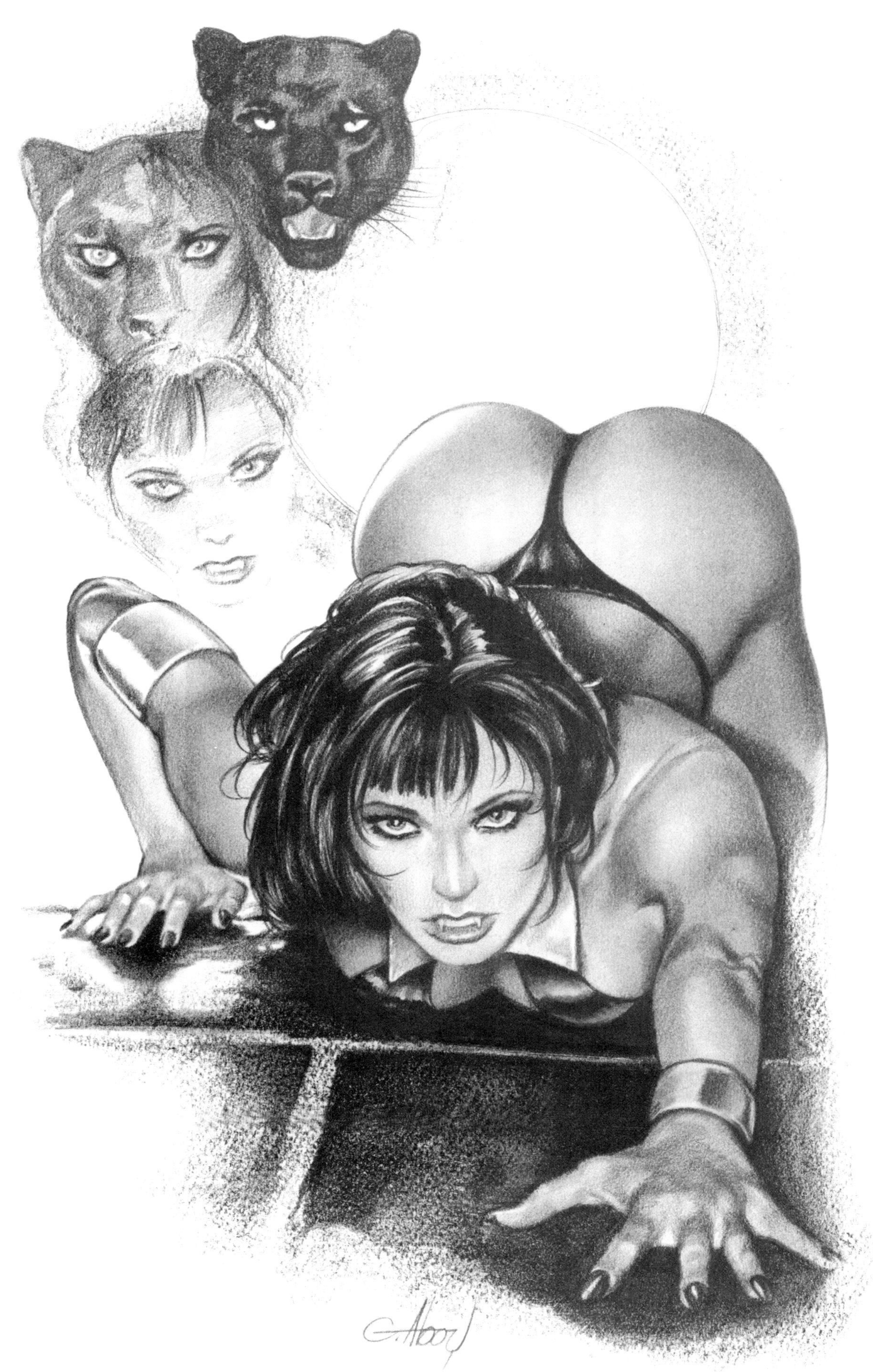

In Touch With Her Wild Side

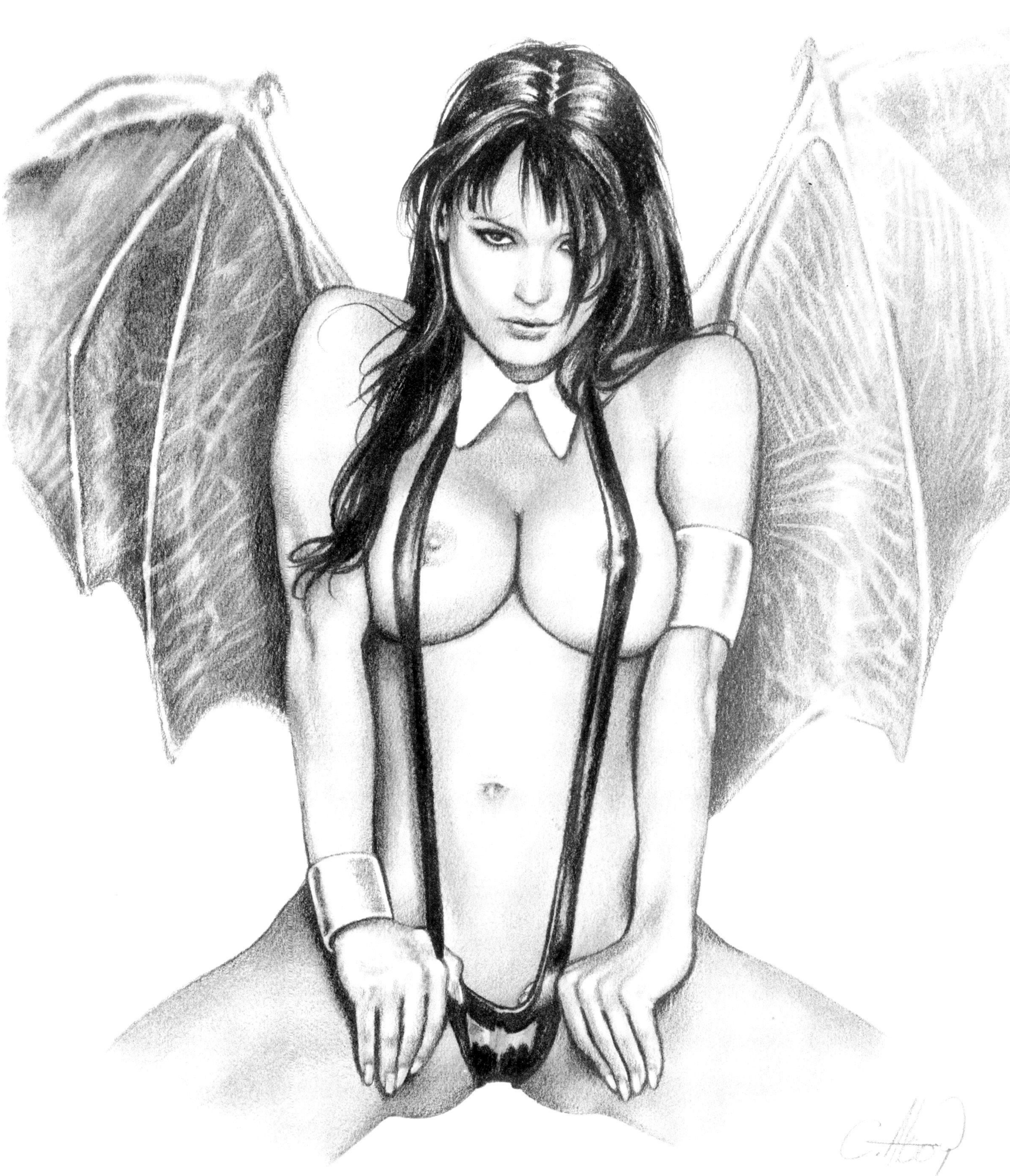

Up All Night For A Reason

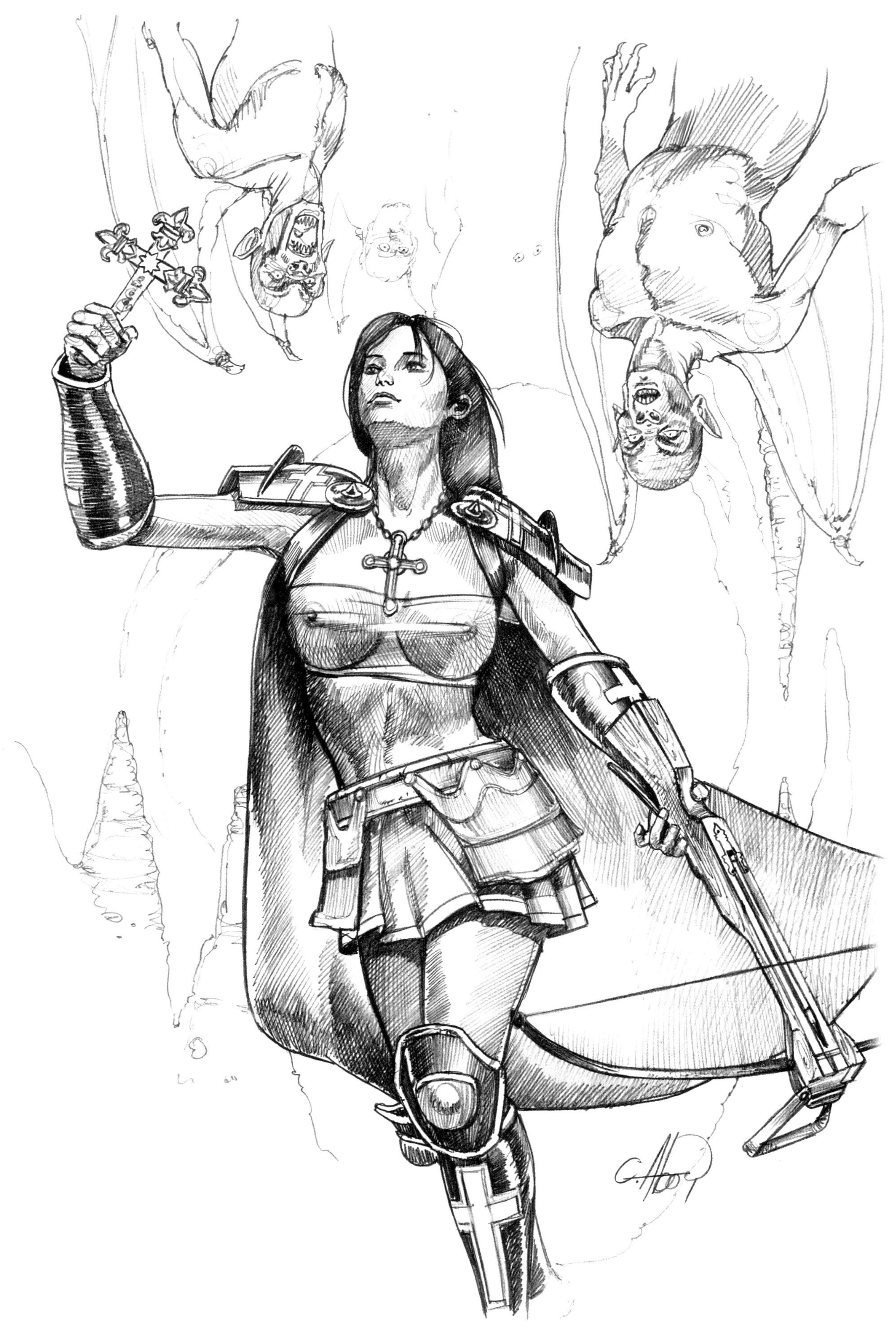

Scourge of Scourges

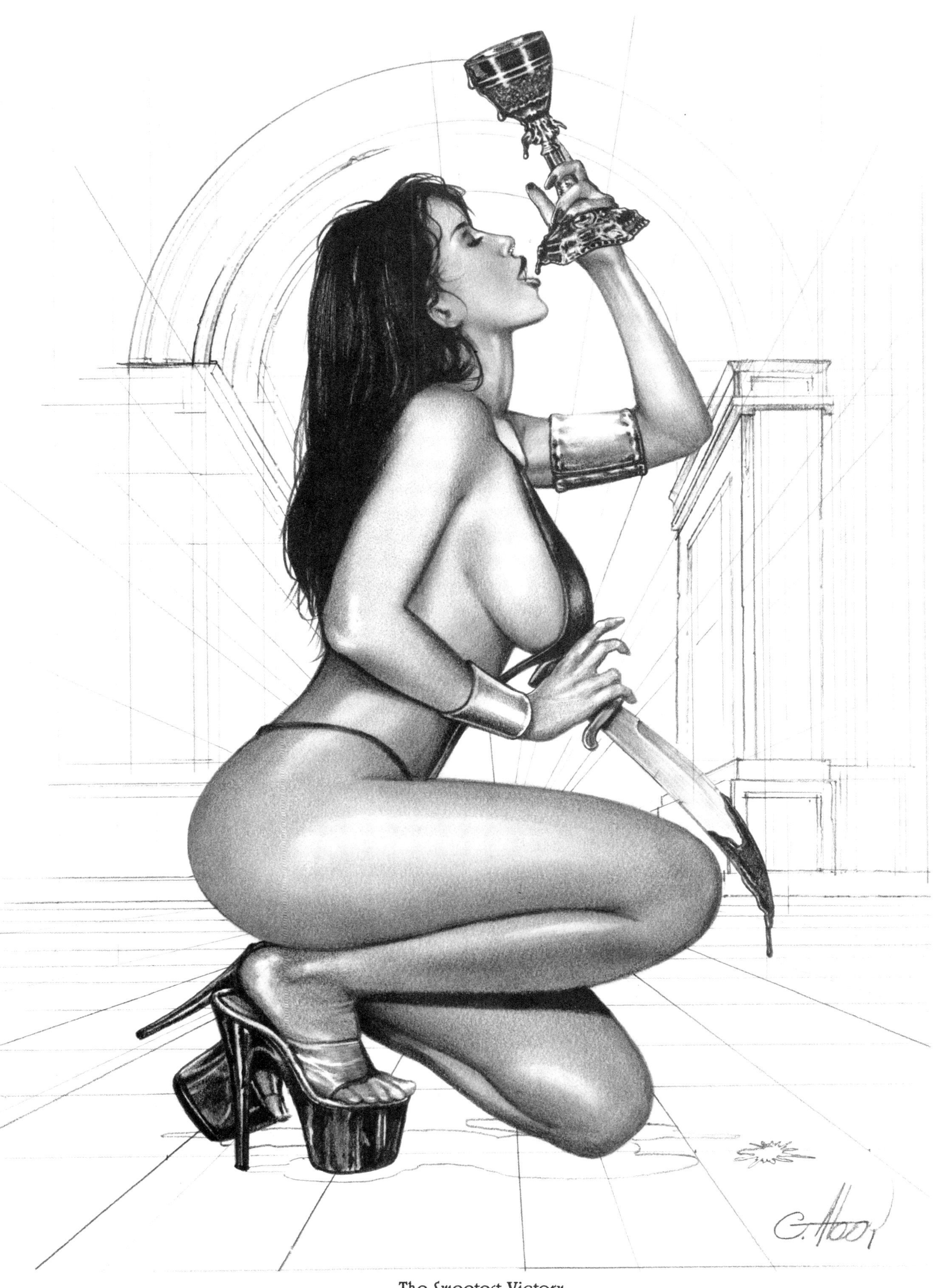

The Sweetest Victory

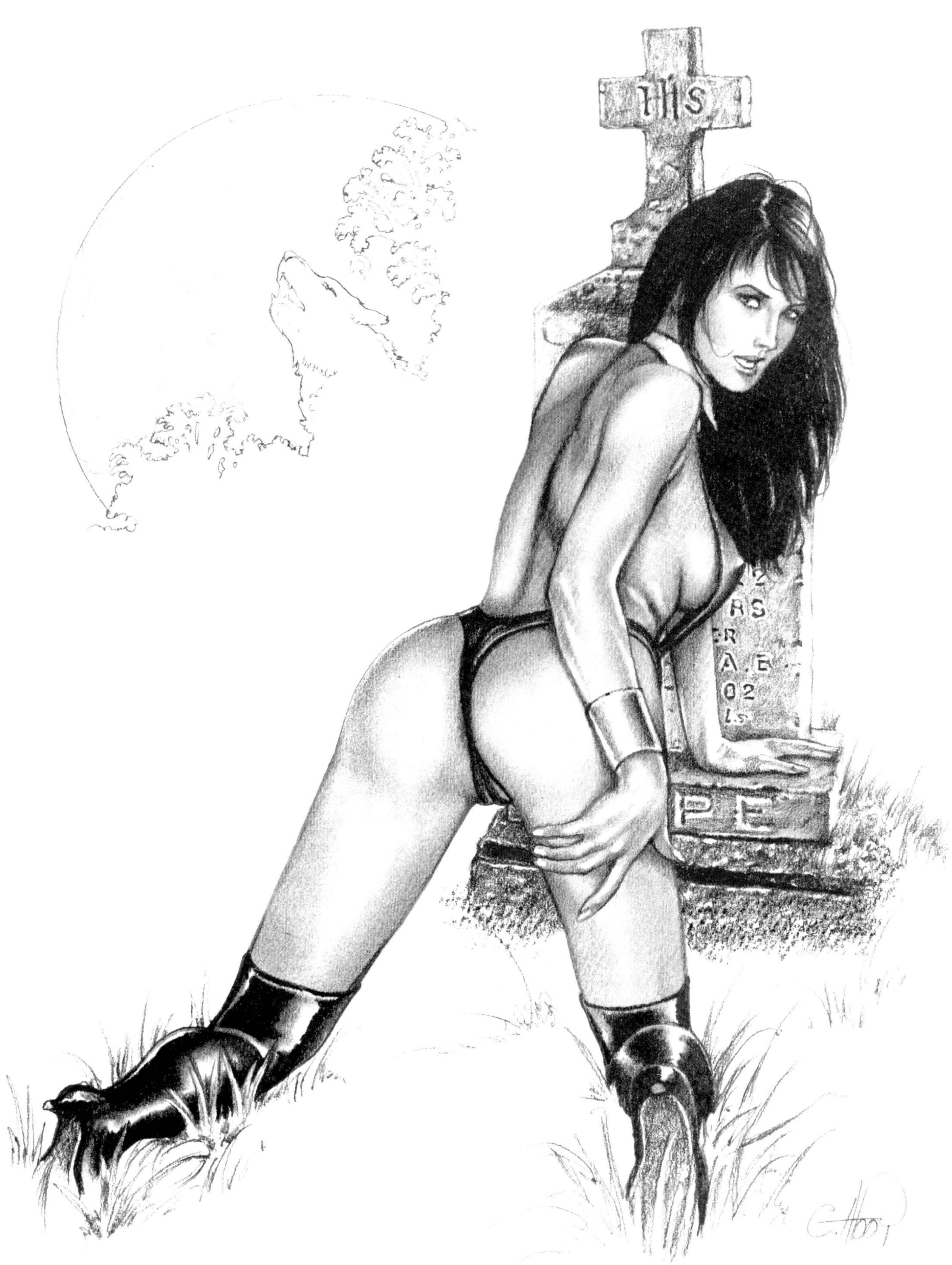

A Tempting Invitation

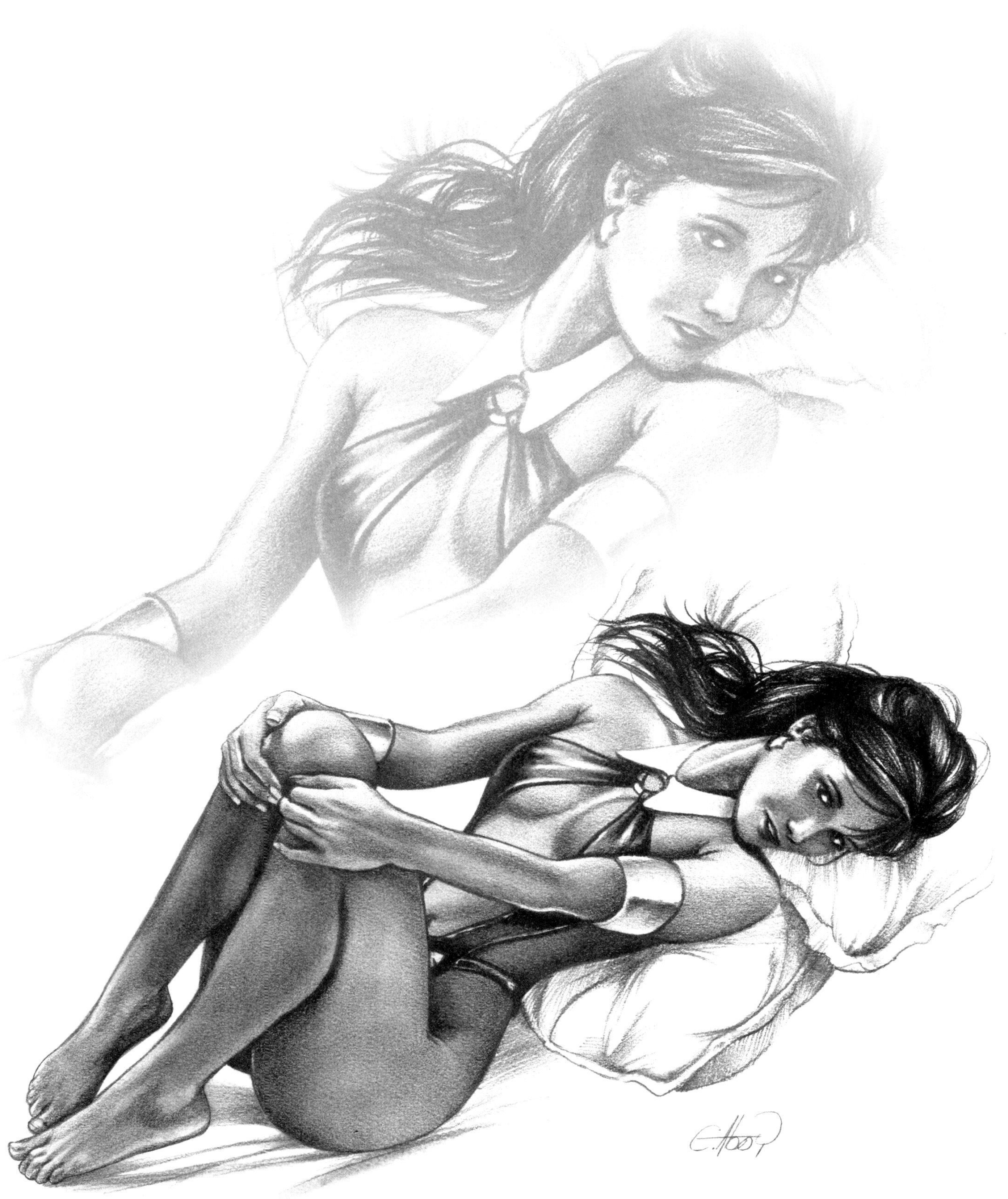

Submit to Damnation

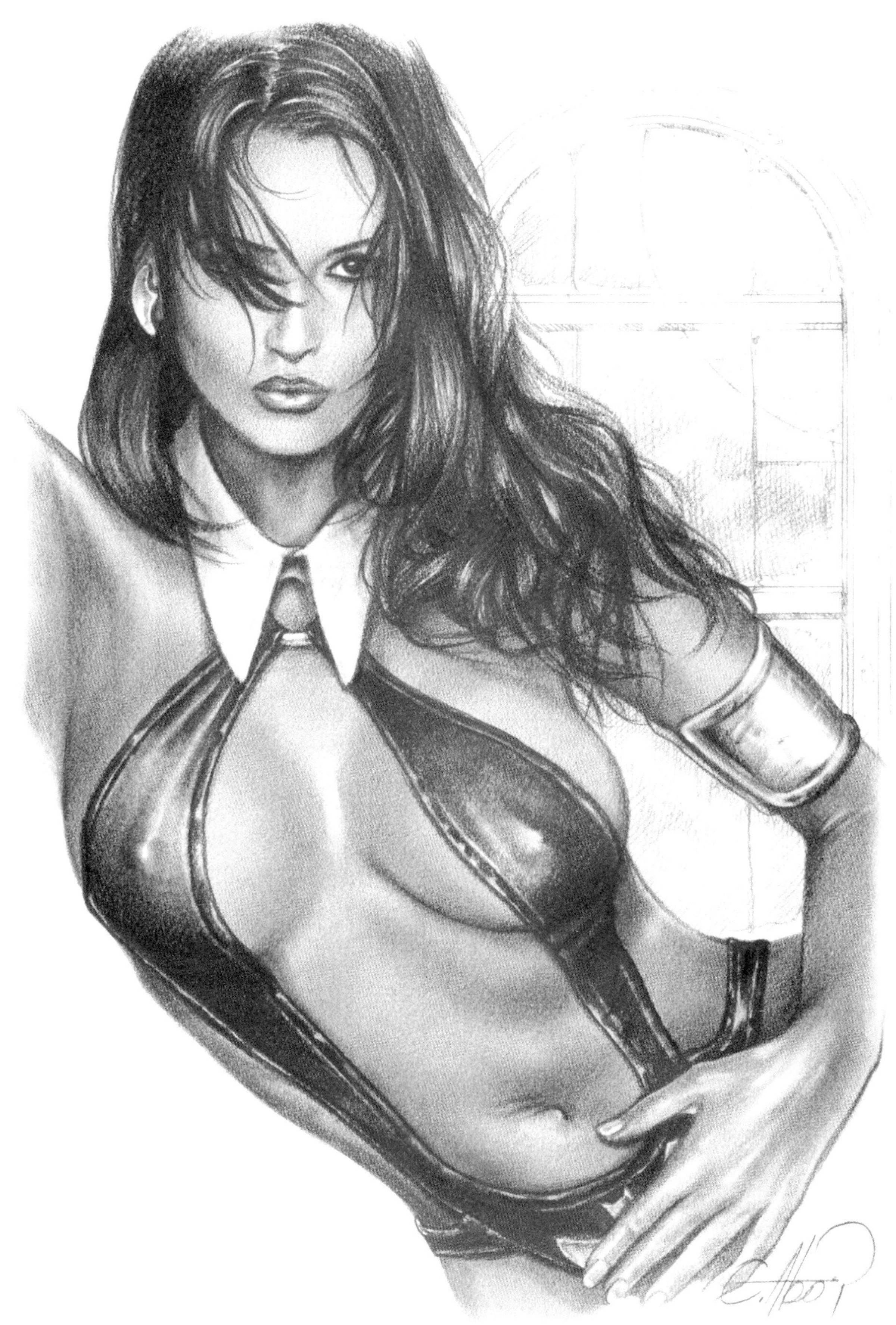

Hunger Pangs

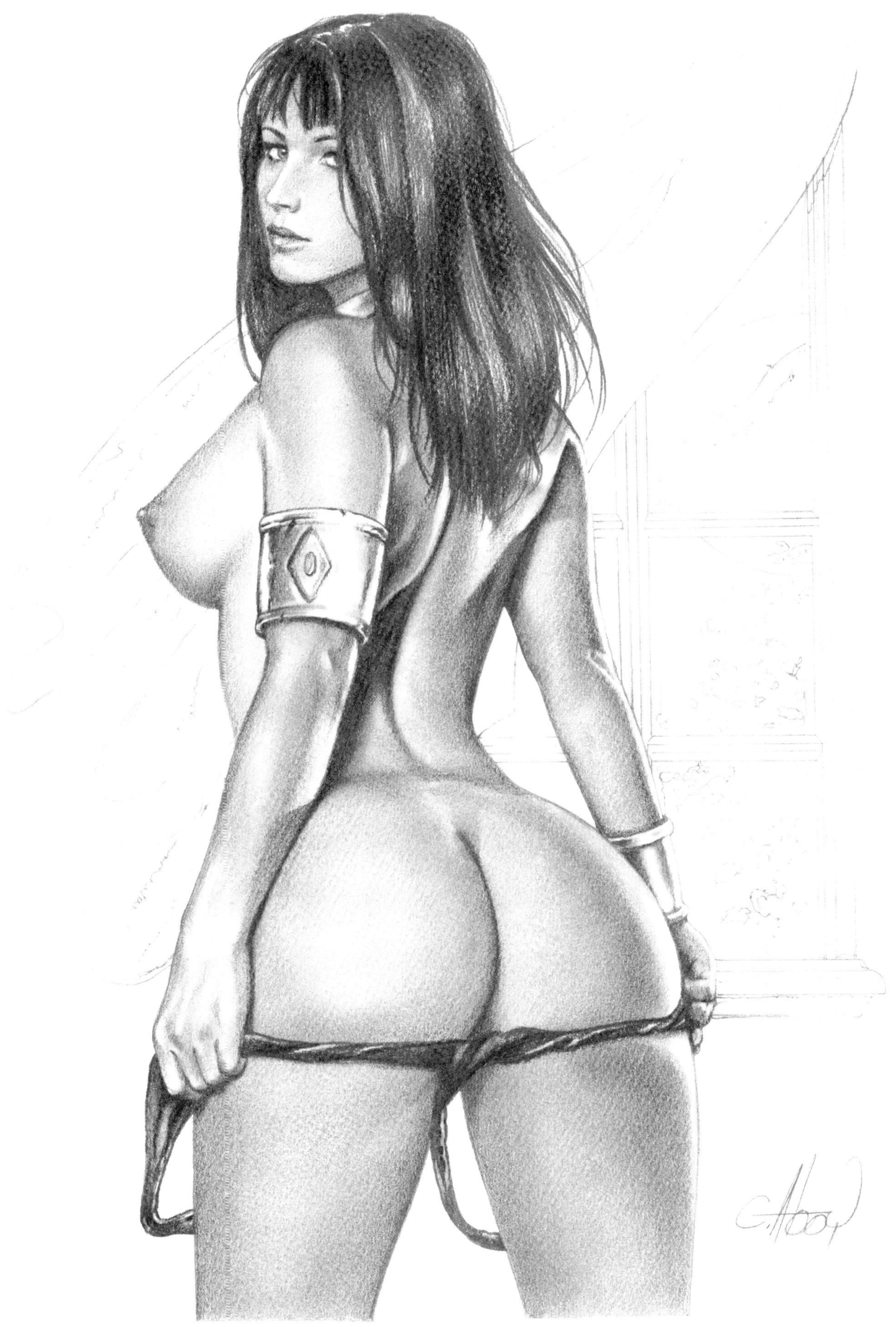

Take A Bite

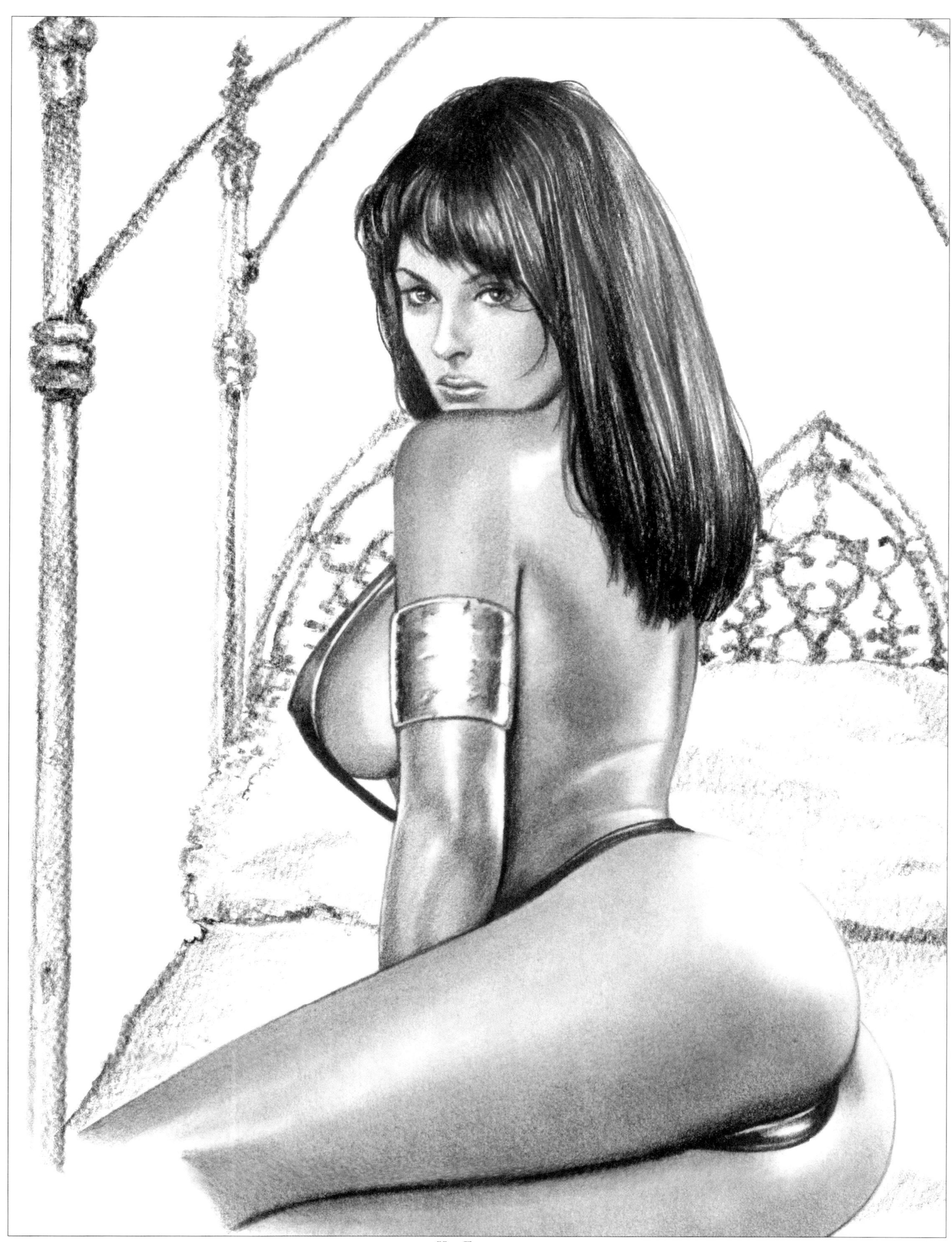

No Escape

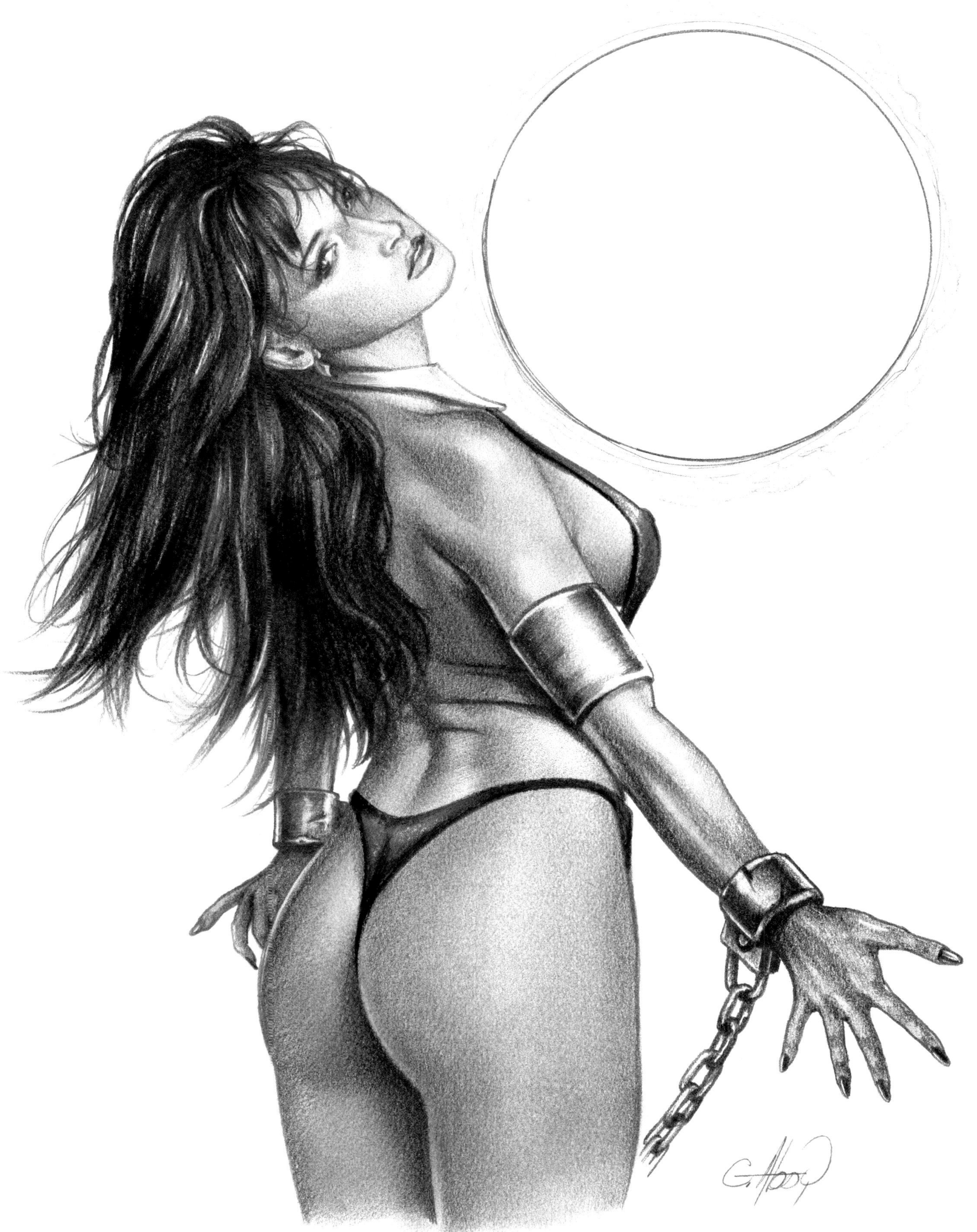

Cruel Prisoner

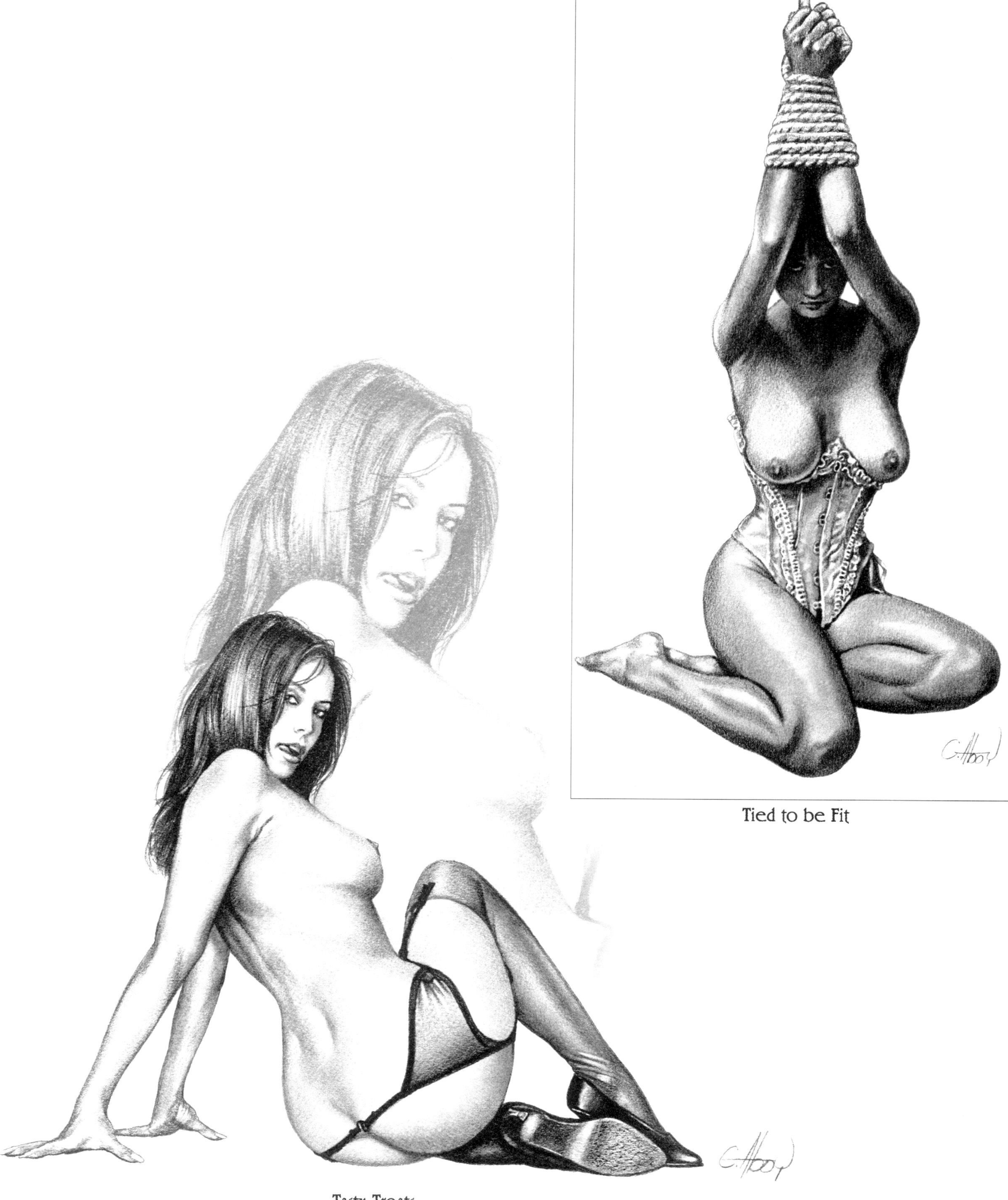

Tied to be Fit

Tasty Treats

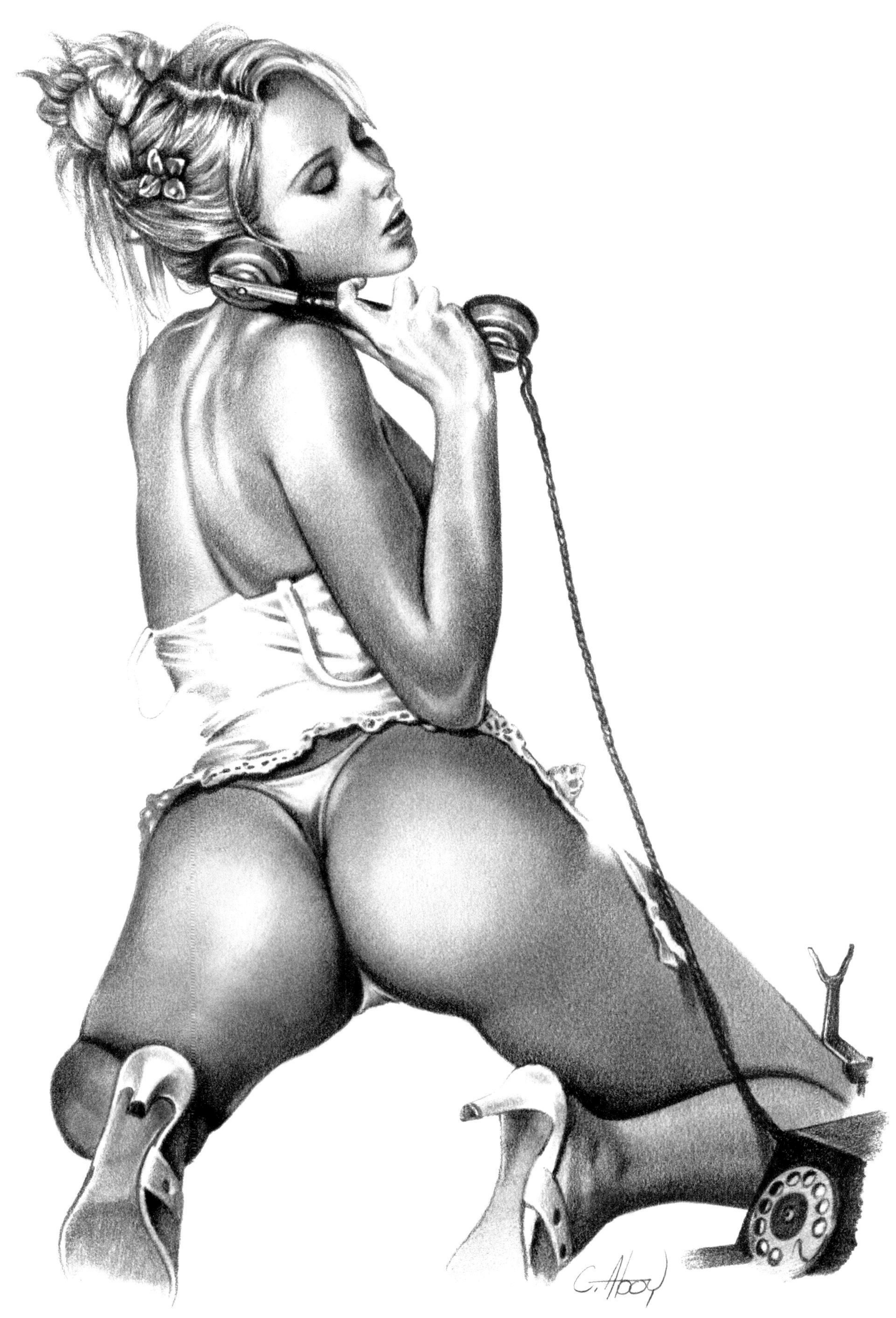

Information...PLEASE!

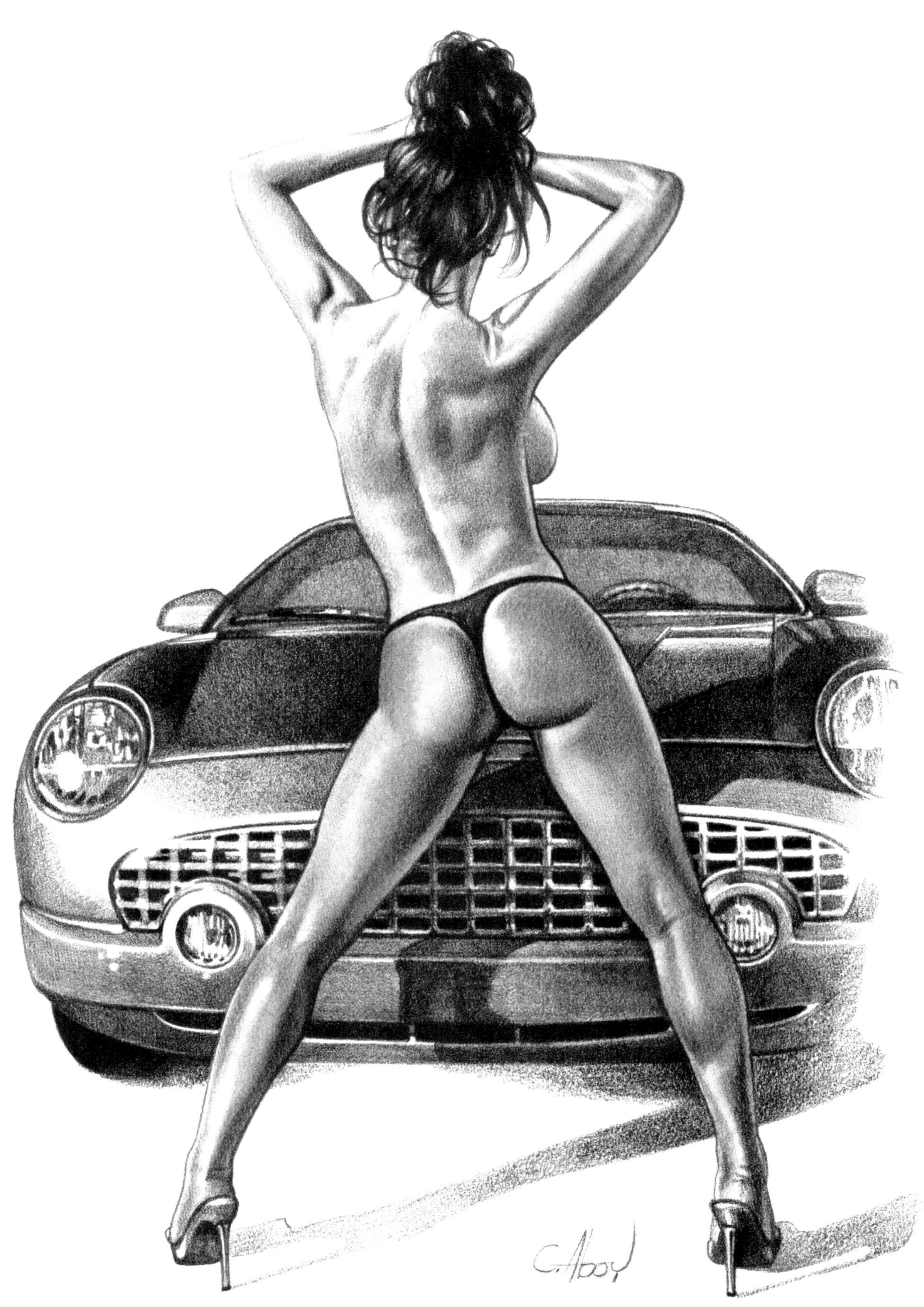

Get Your Motors Running...

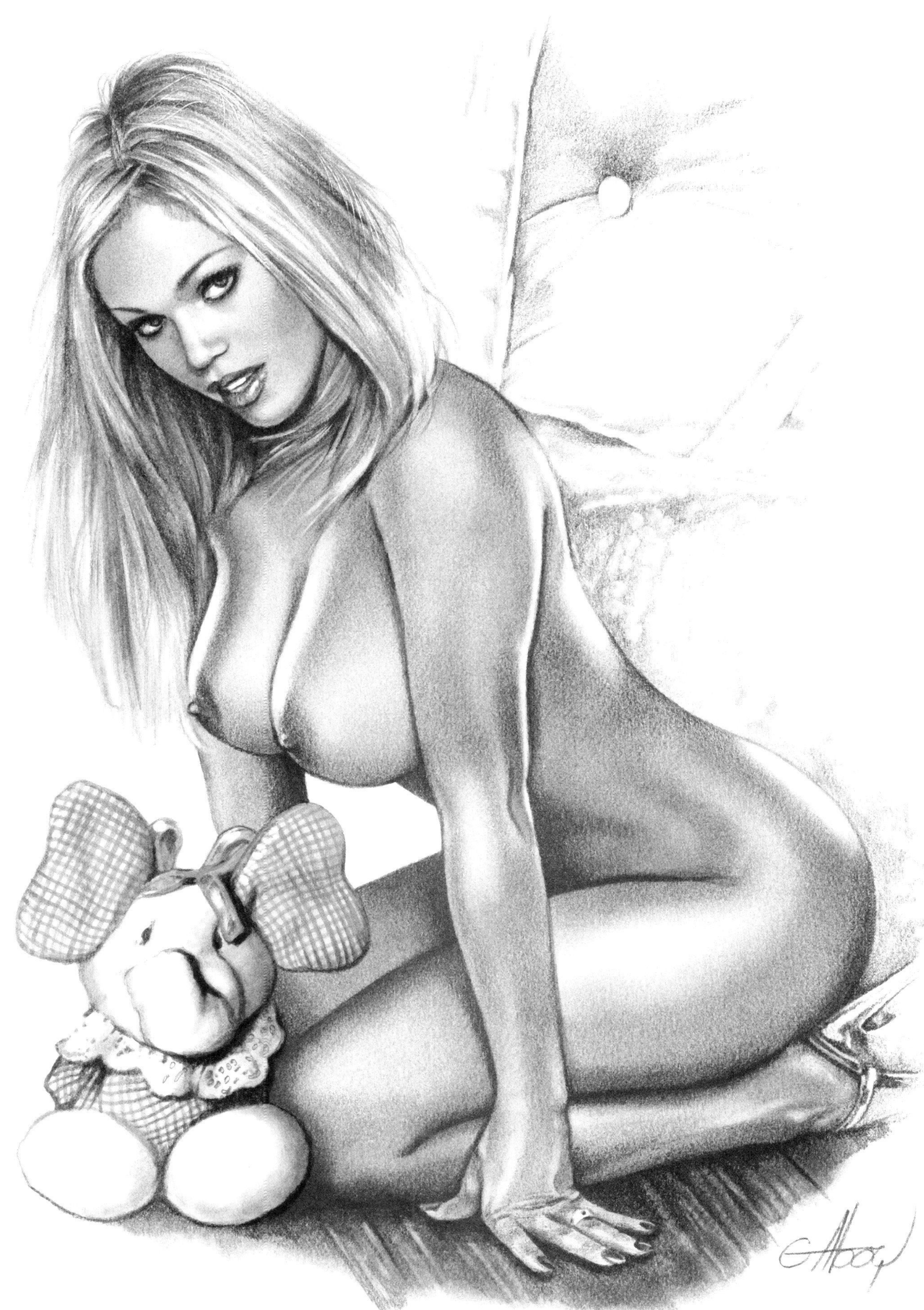

Baby Doll Never Forgets

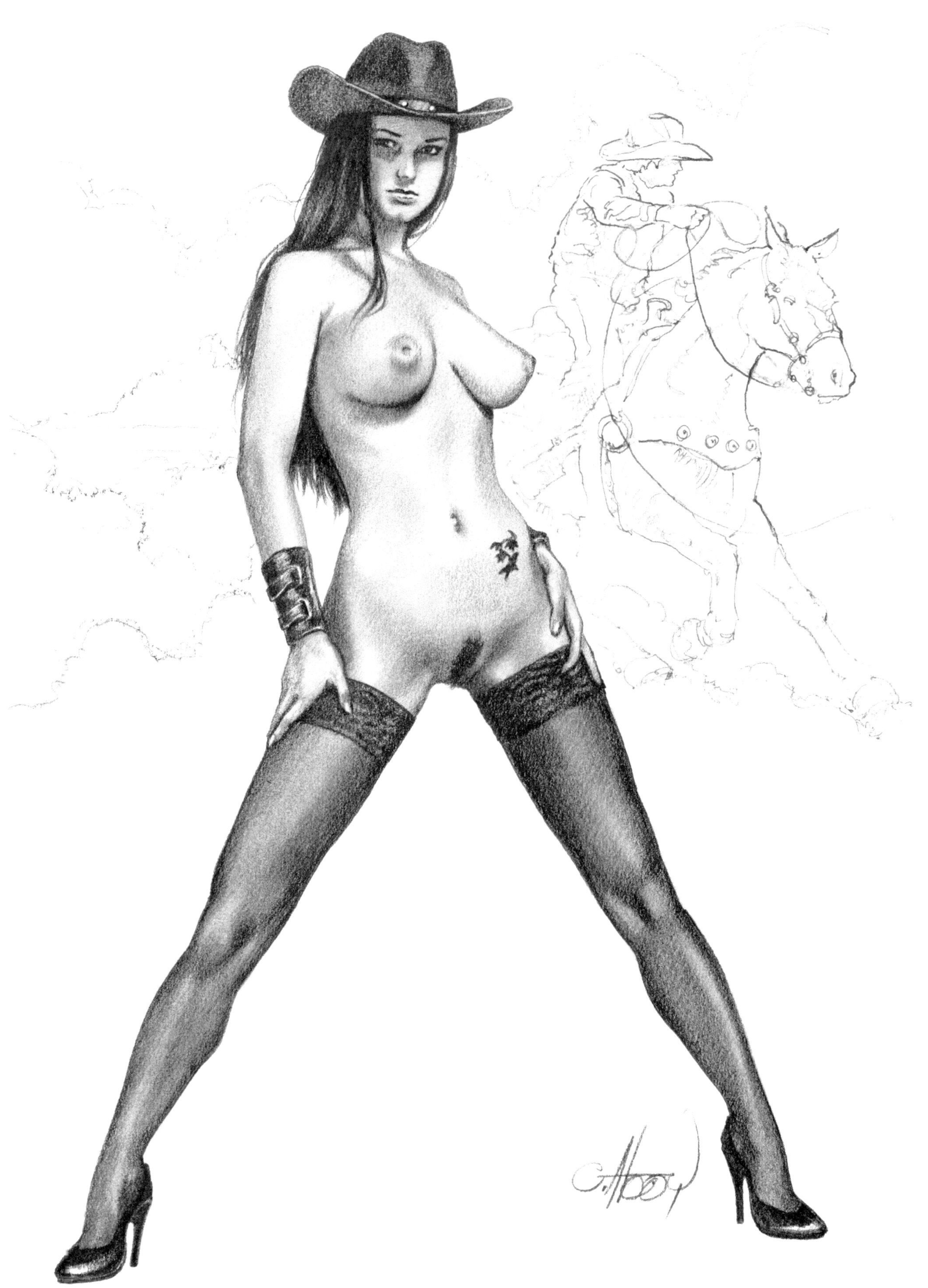

South of the Rio Grande!

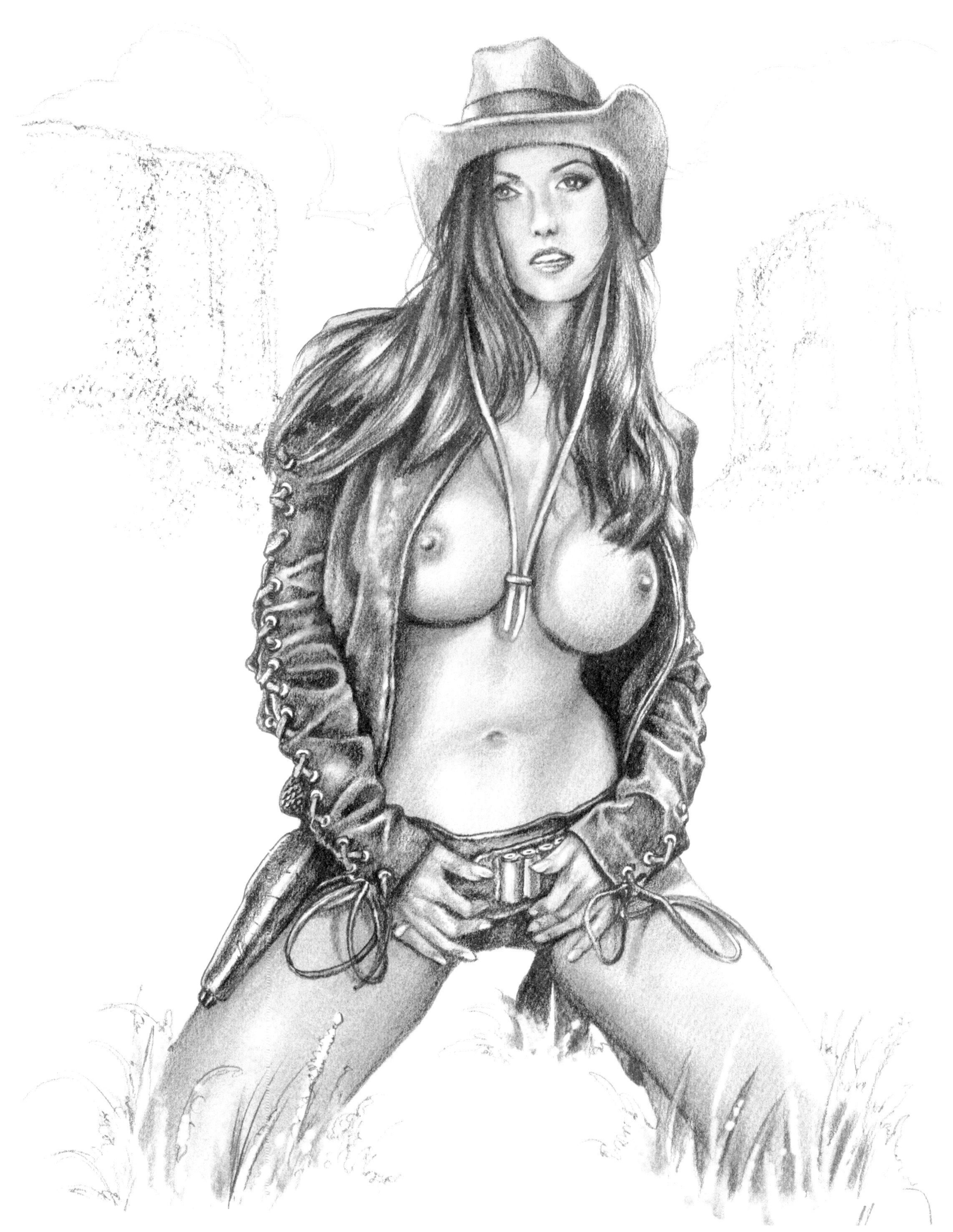

Very Wide Open Spaces

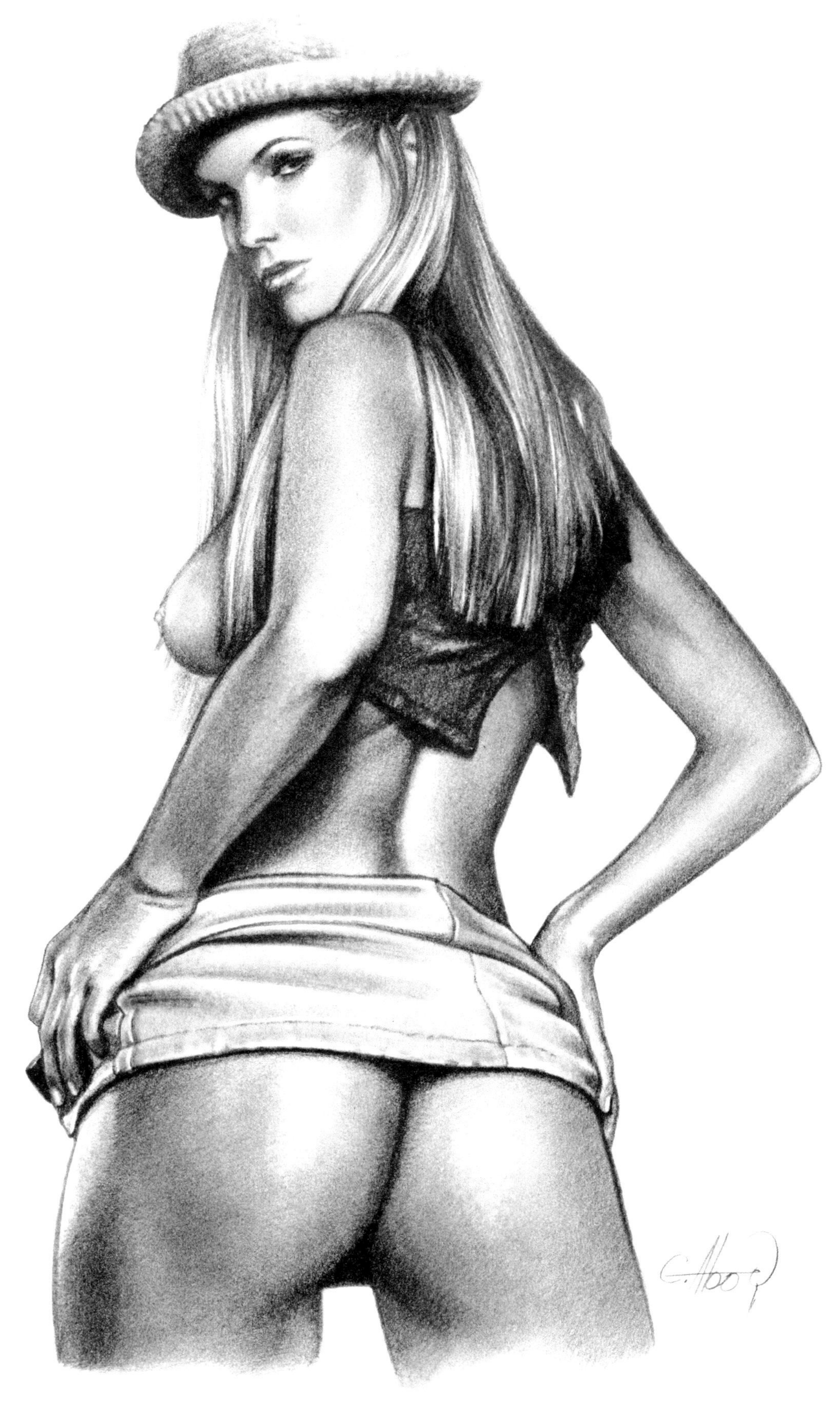

Ride On Up!

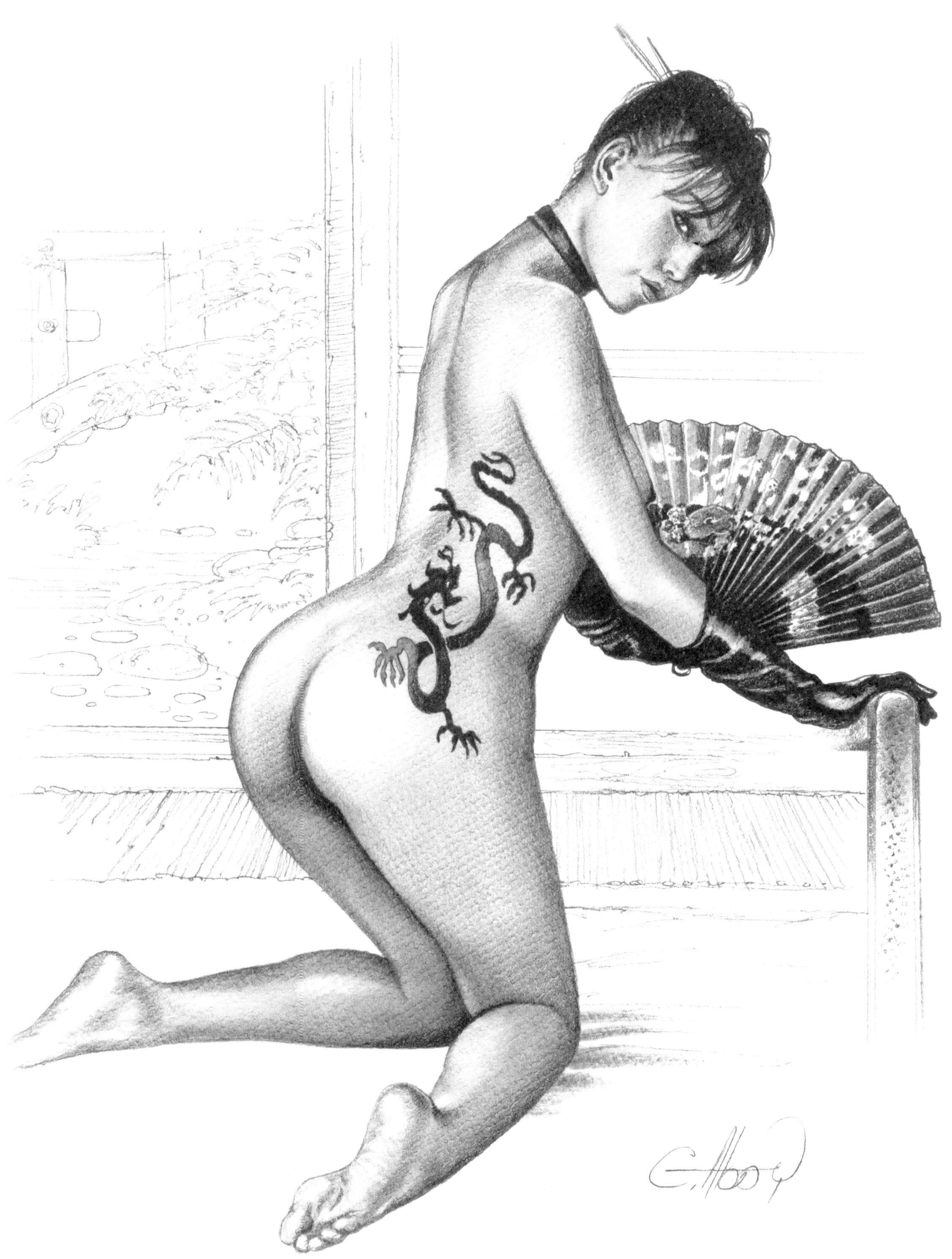

Chase THIS Dragon

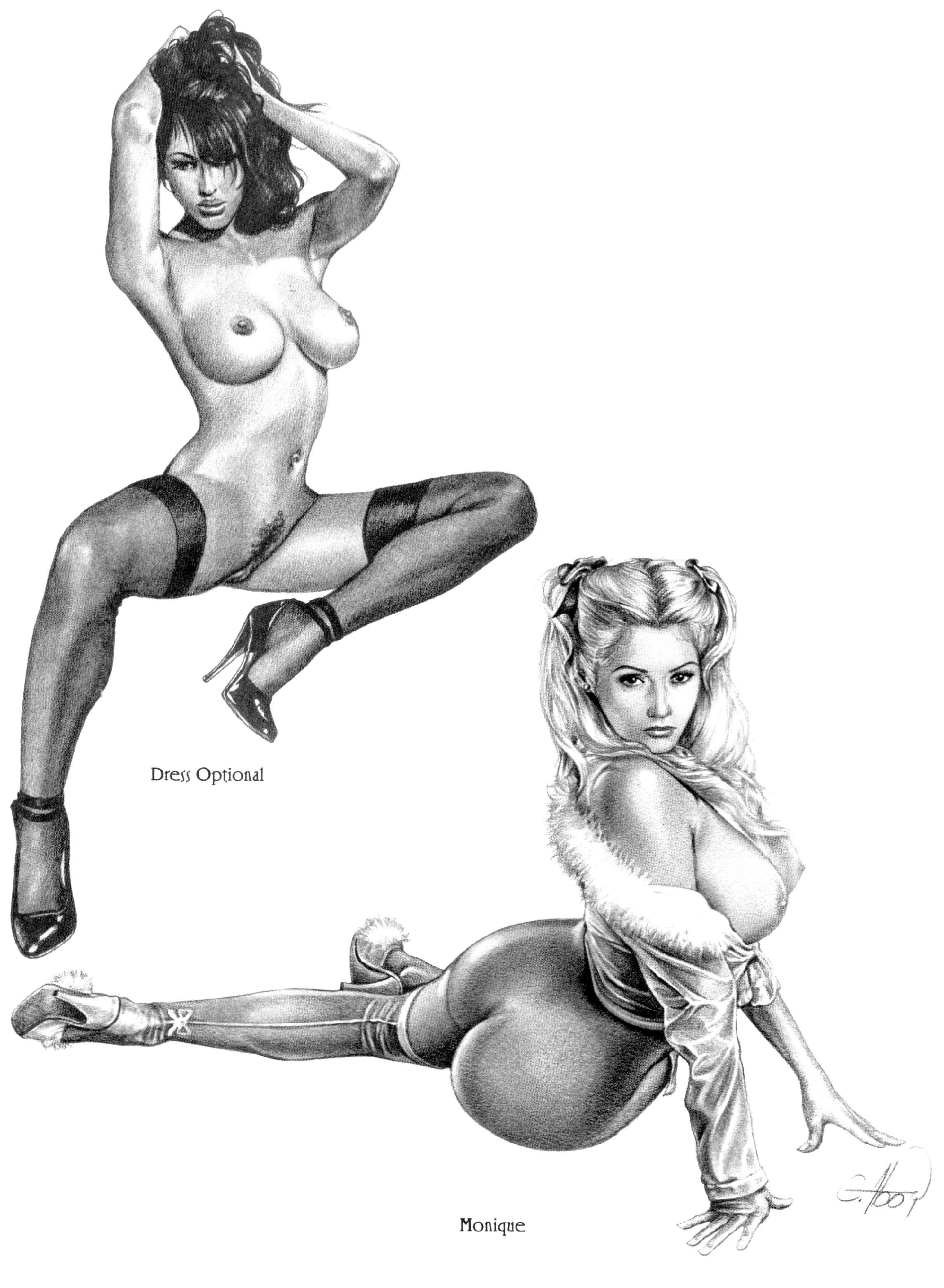

Dress Optional

Monique

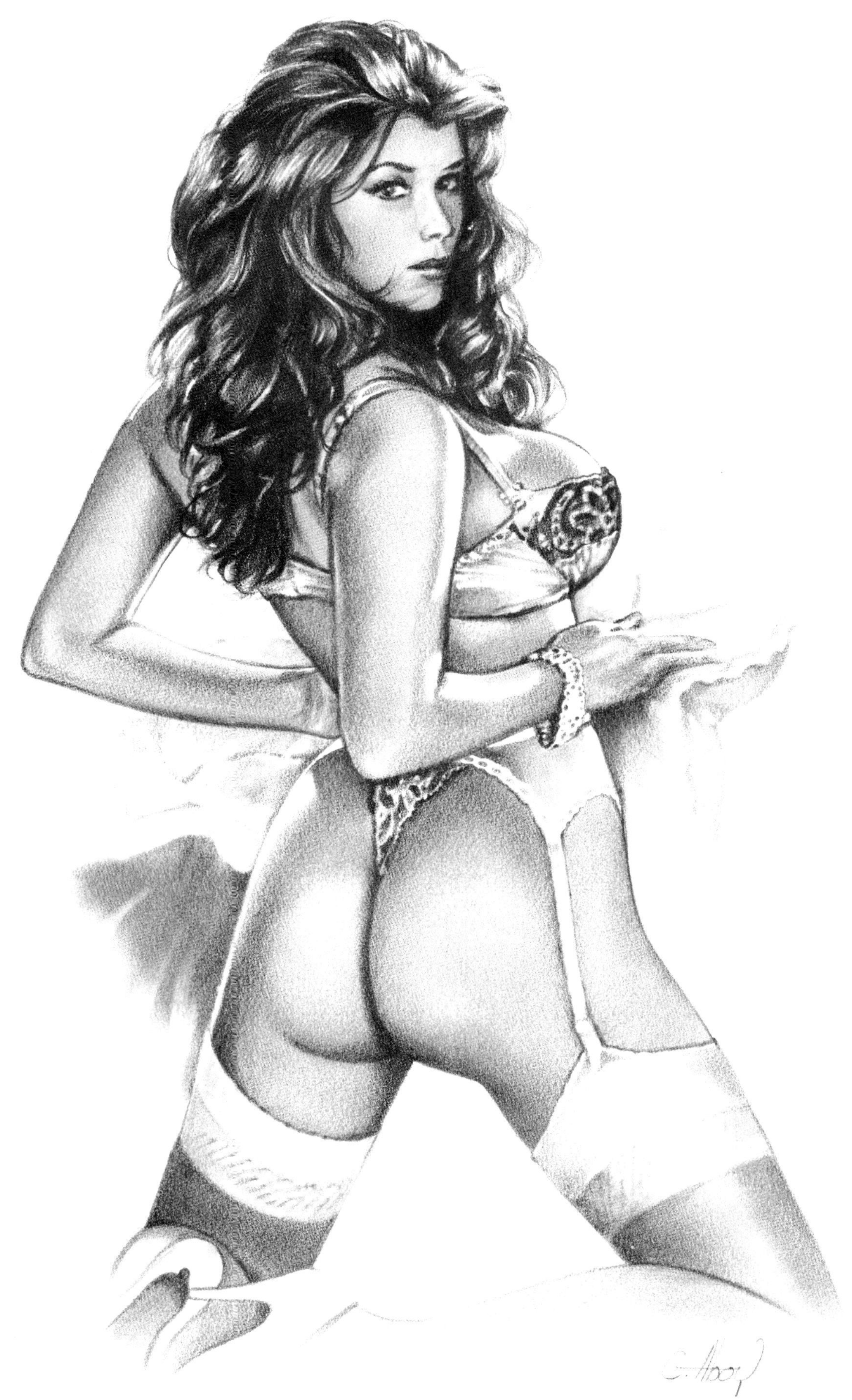

Unforgettable

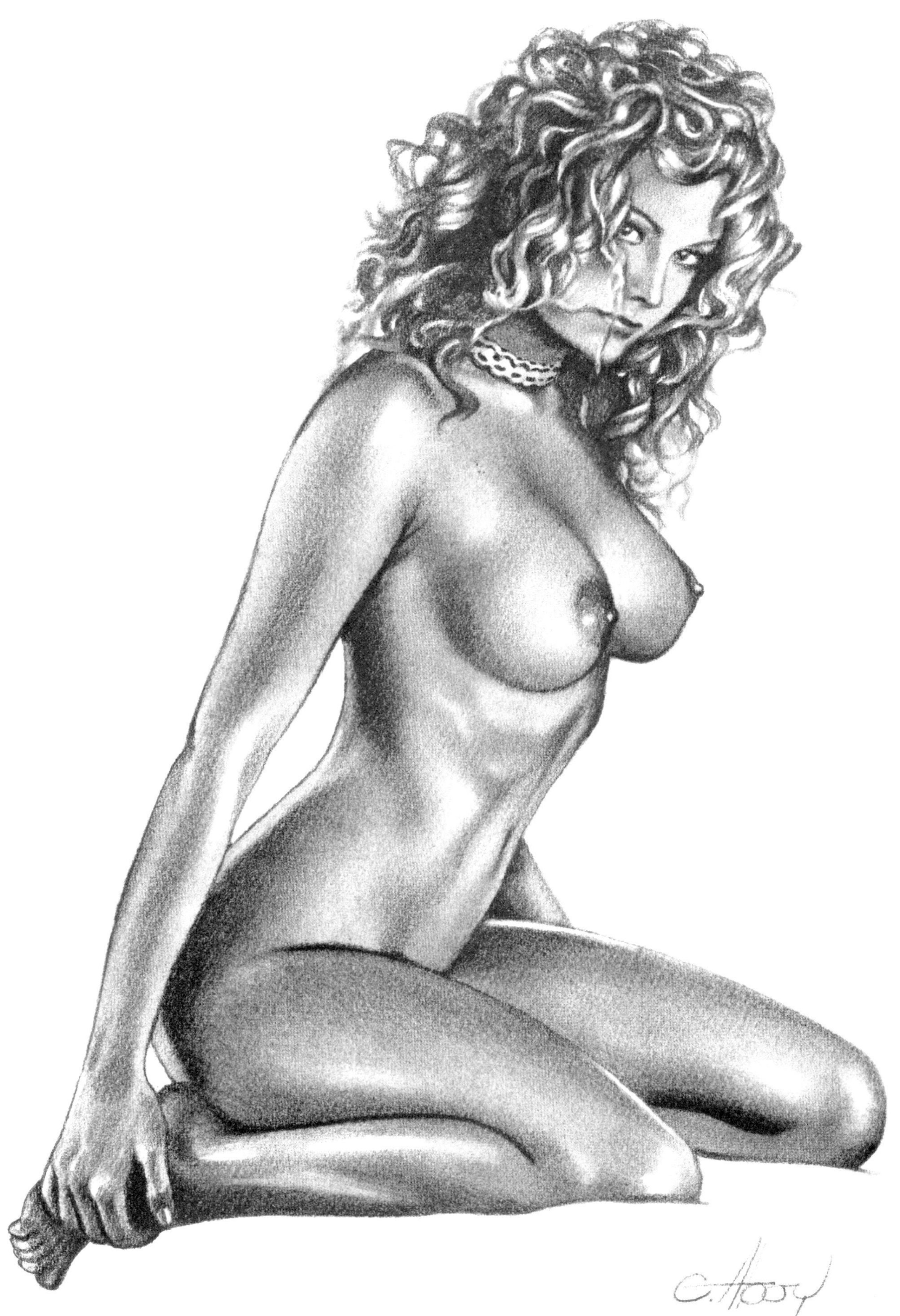

Roxanne

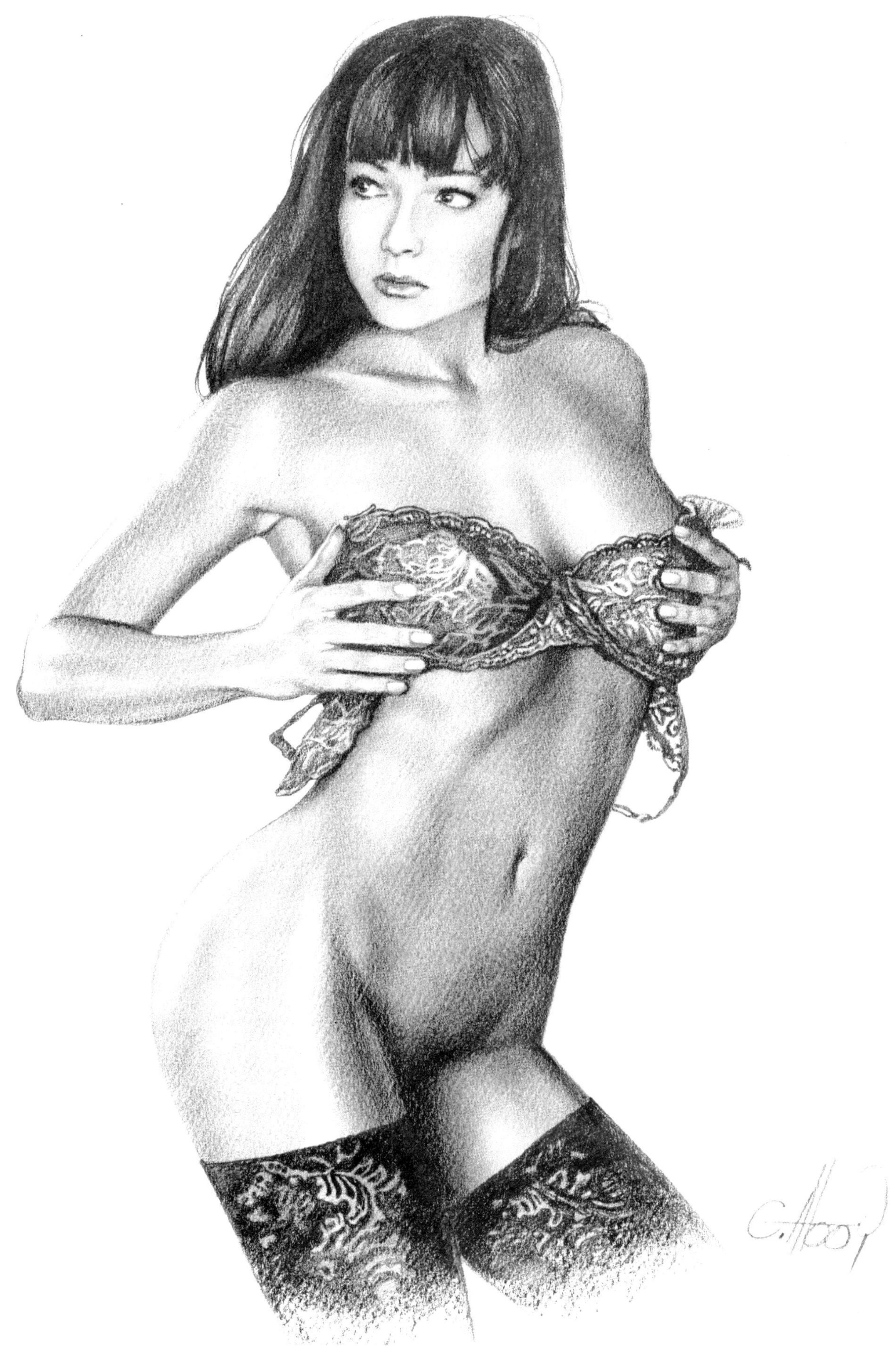

Yvette

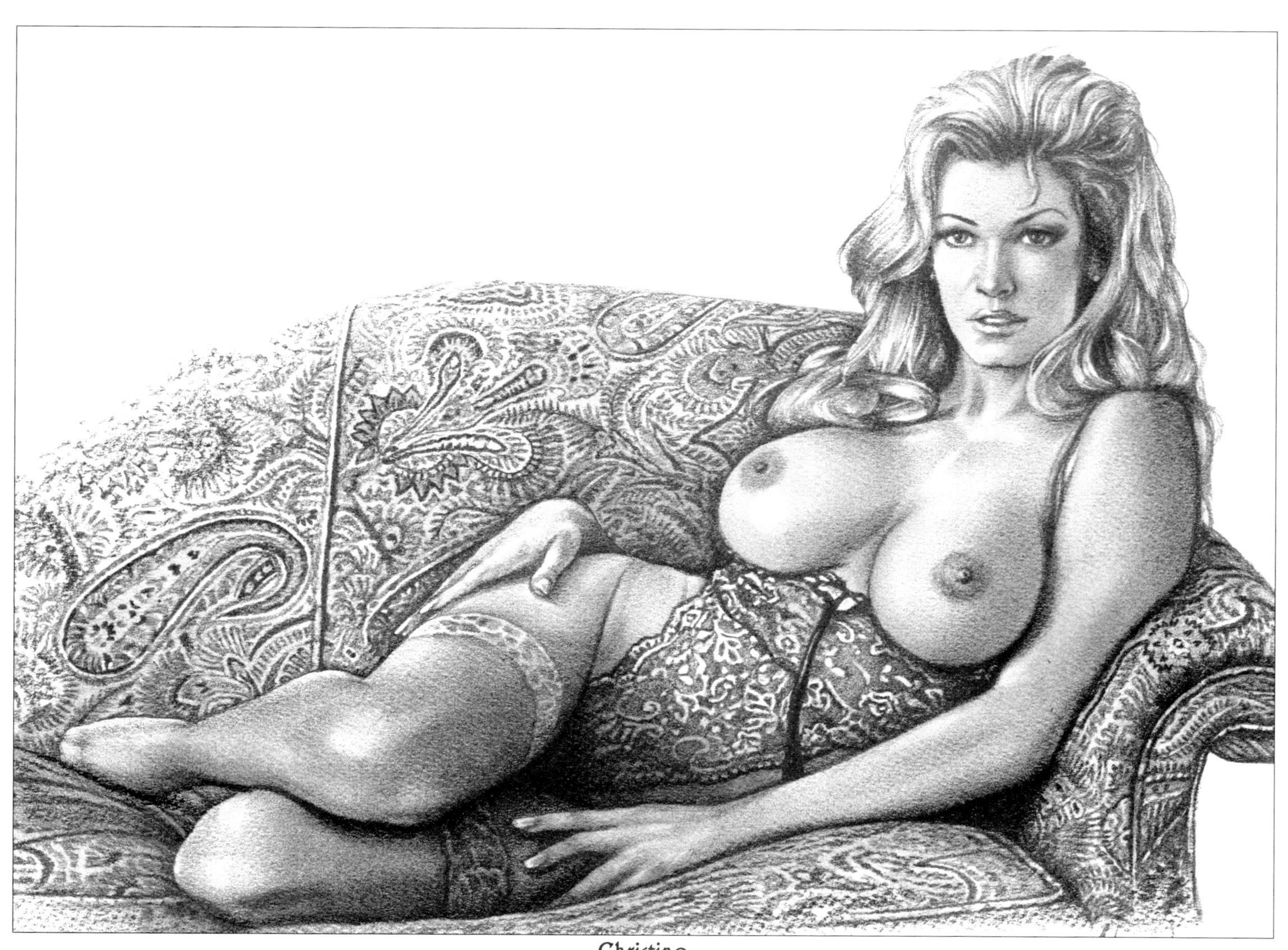

Christine

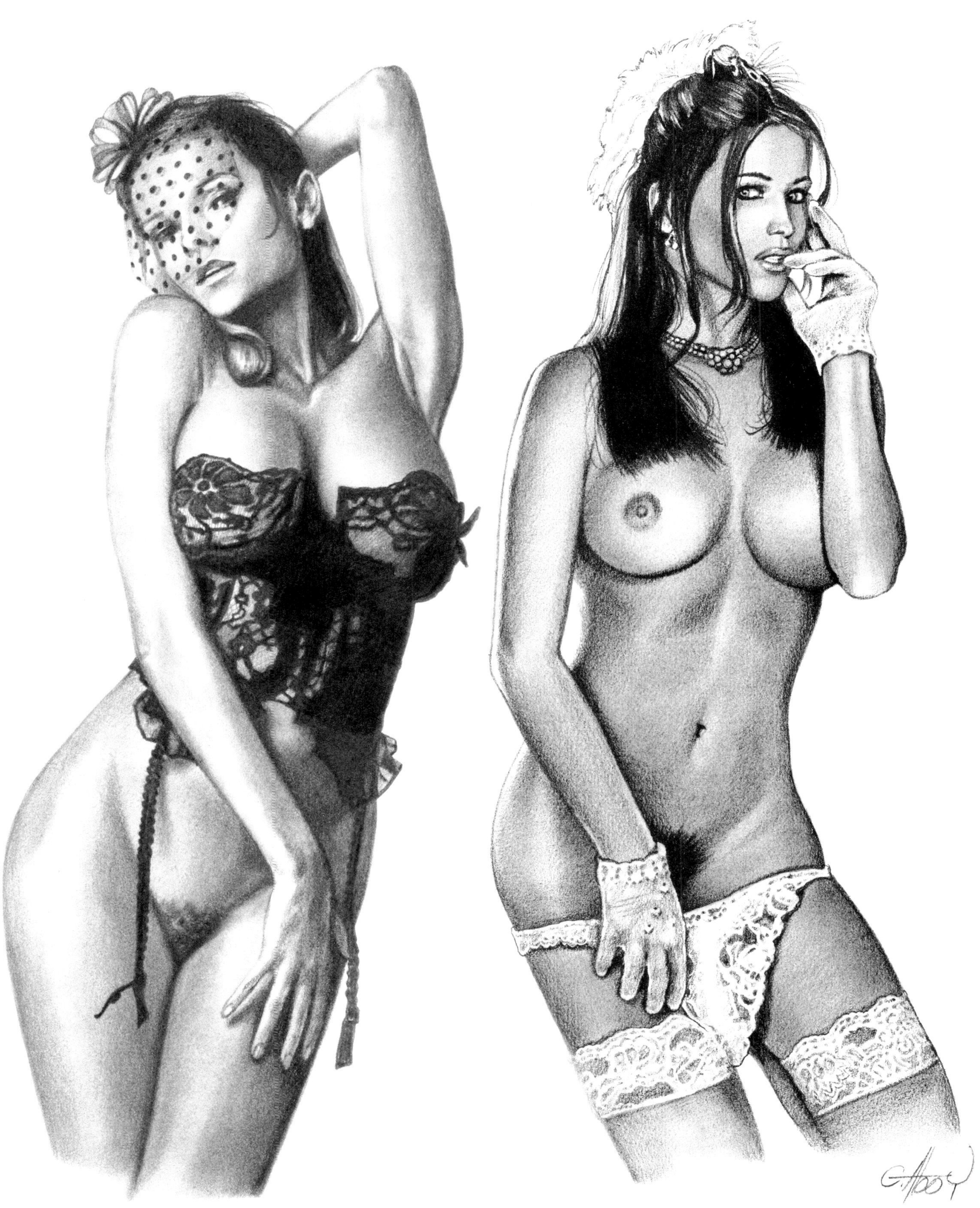

Very Naughty and Very Nice

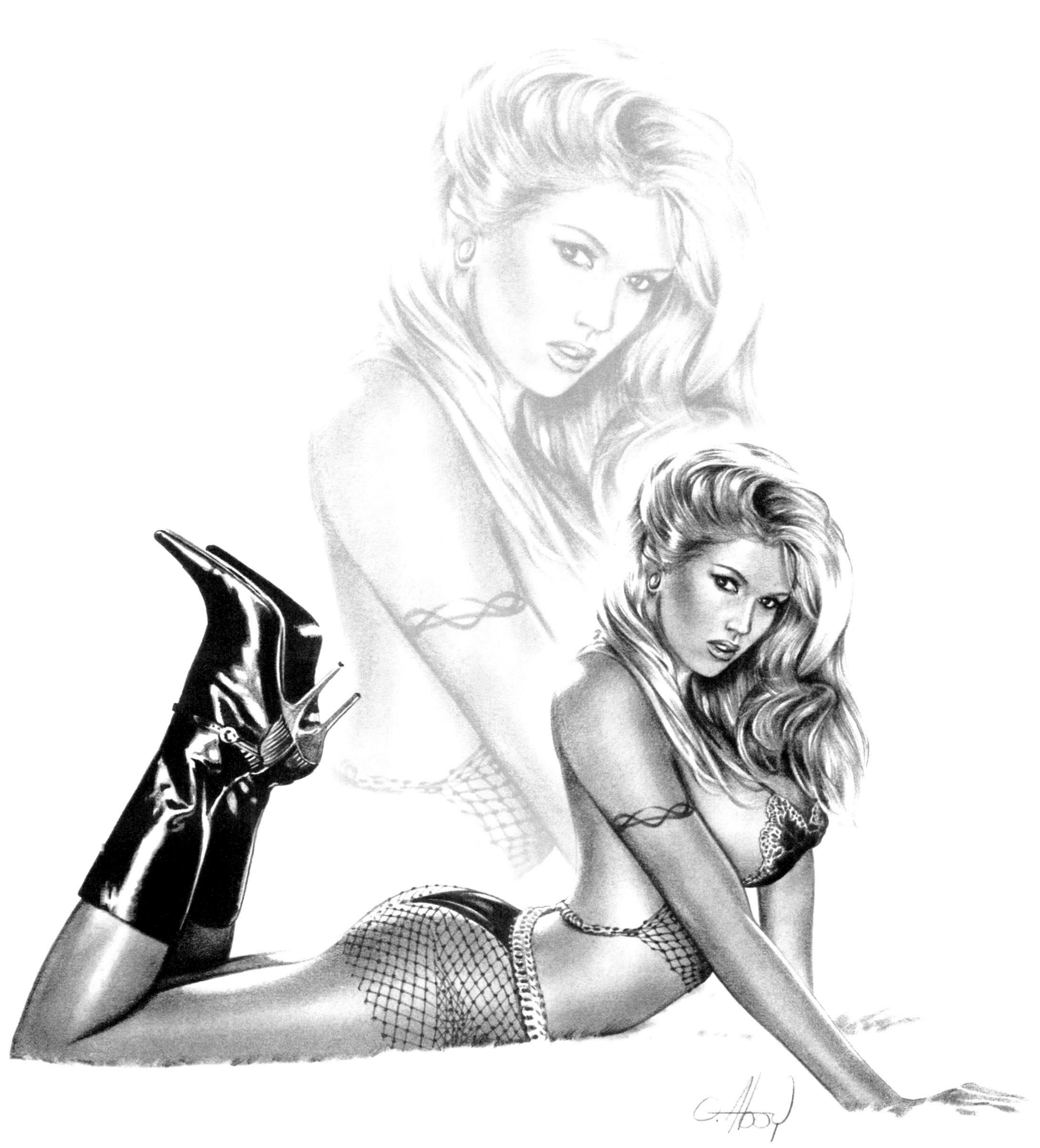

Shiny Boots

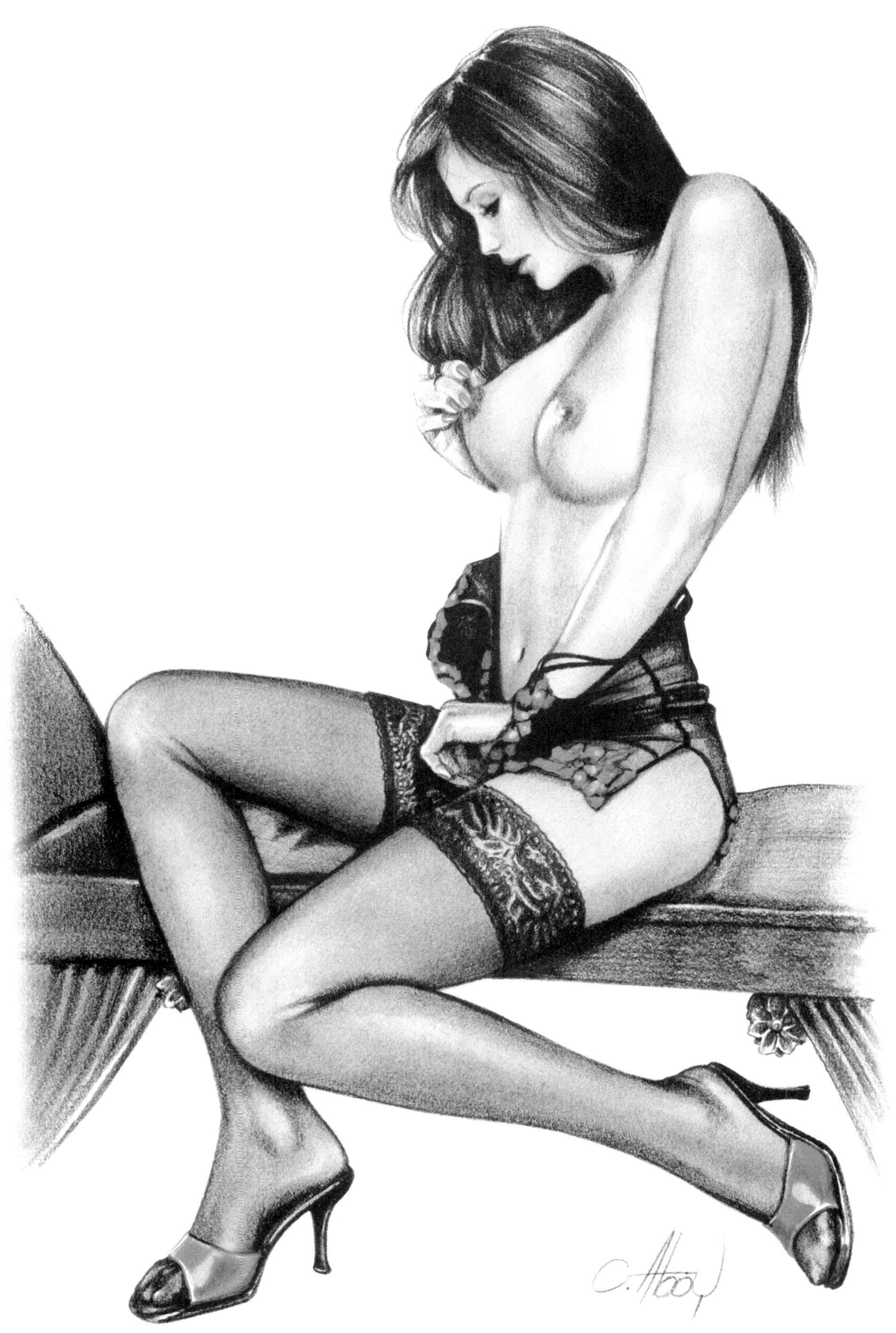

Undressing Room

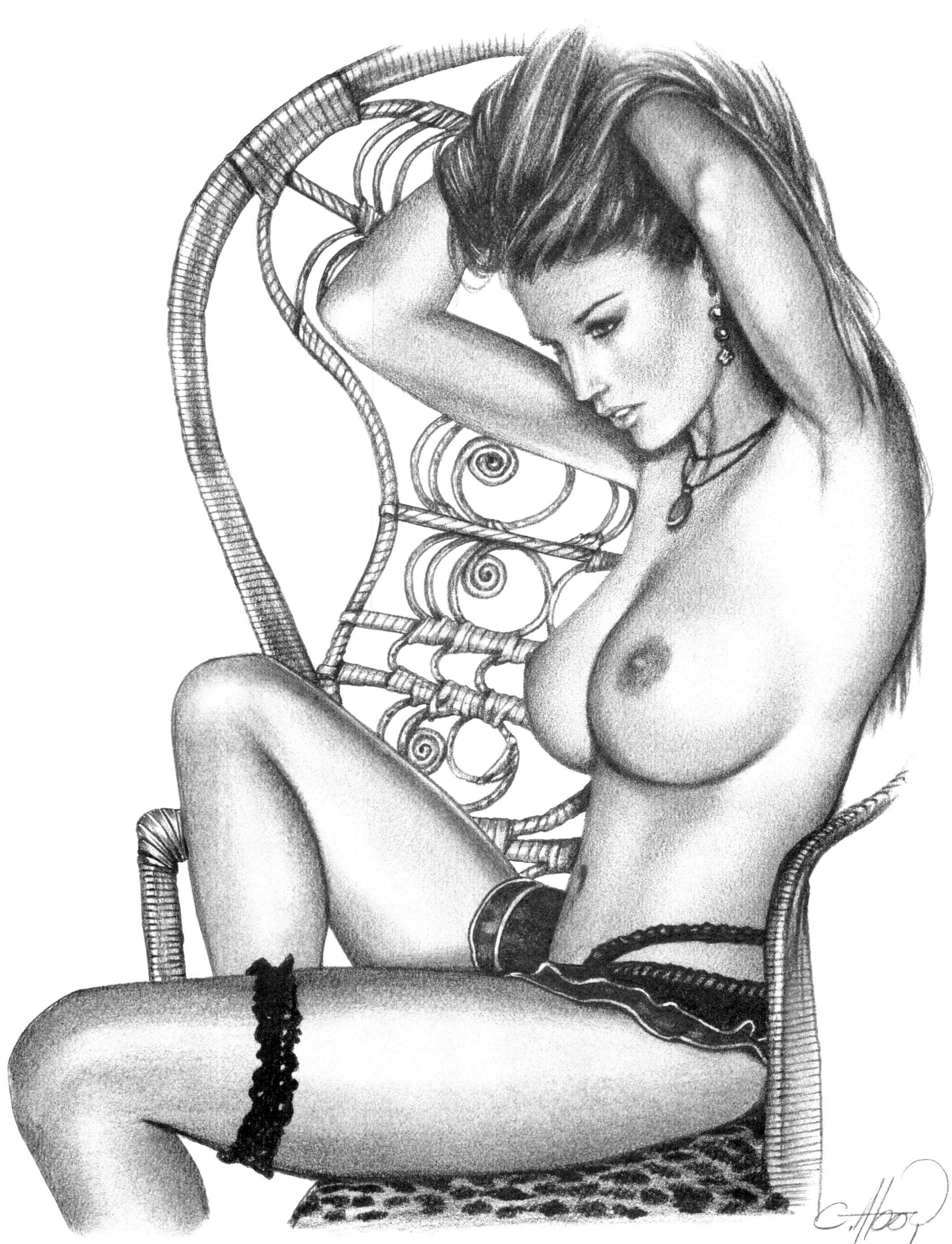

Talia

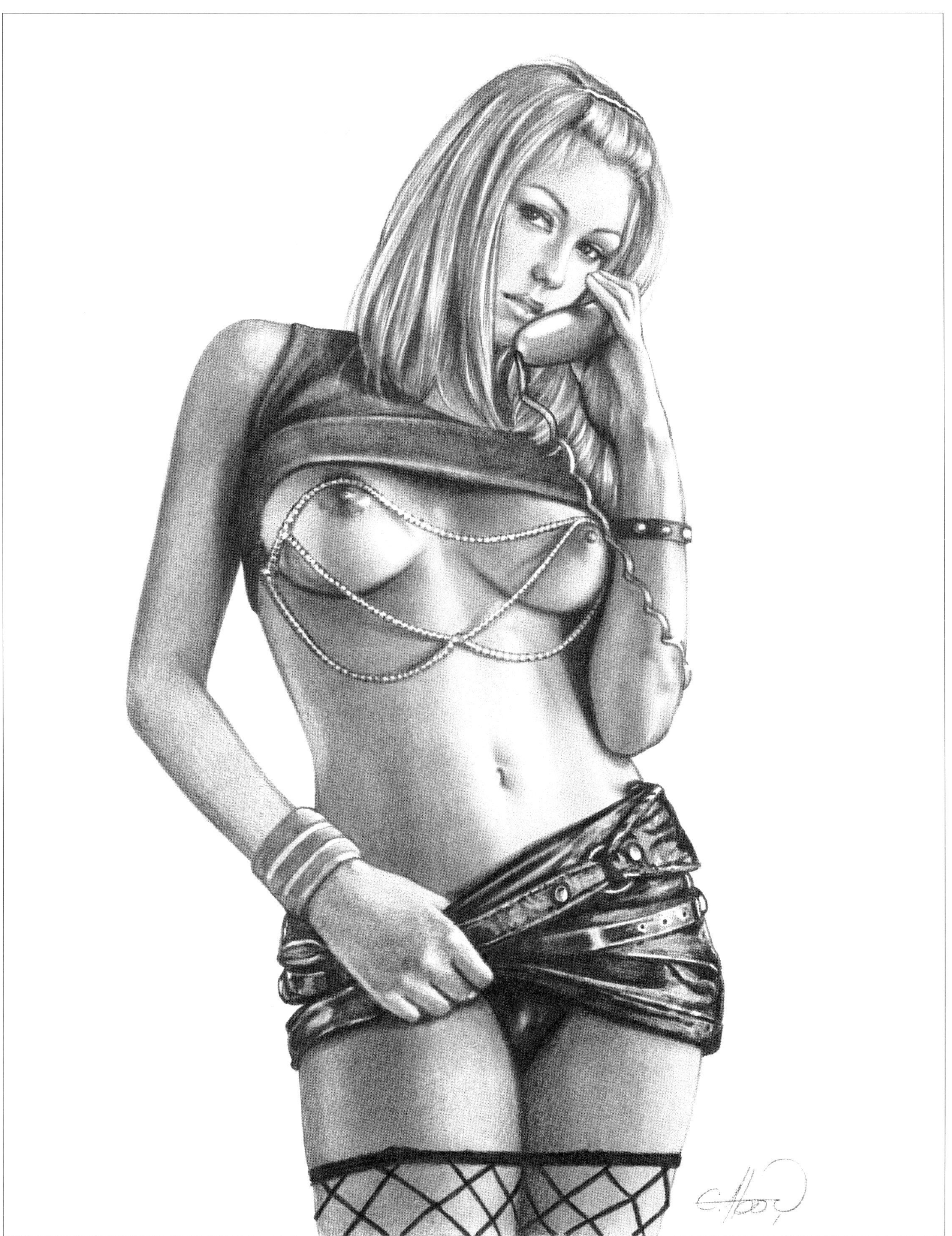

"What are YOU wearing?"

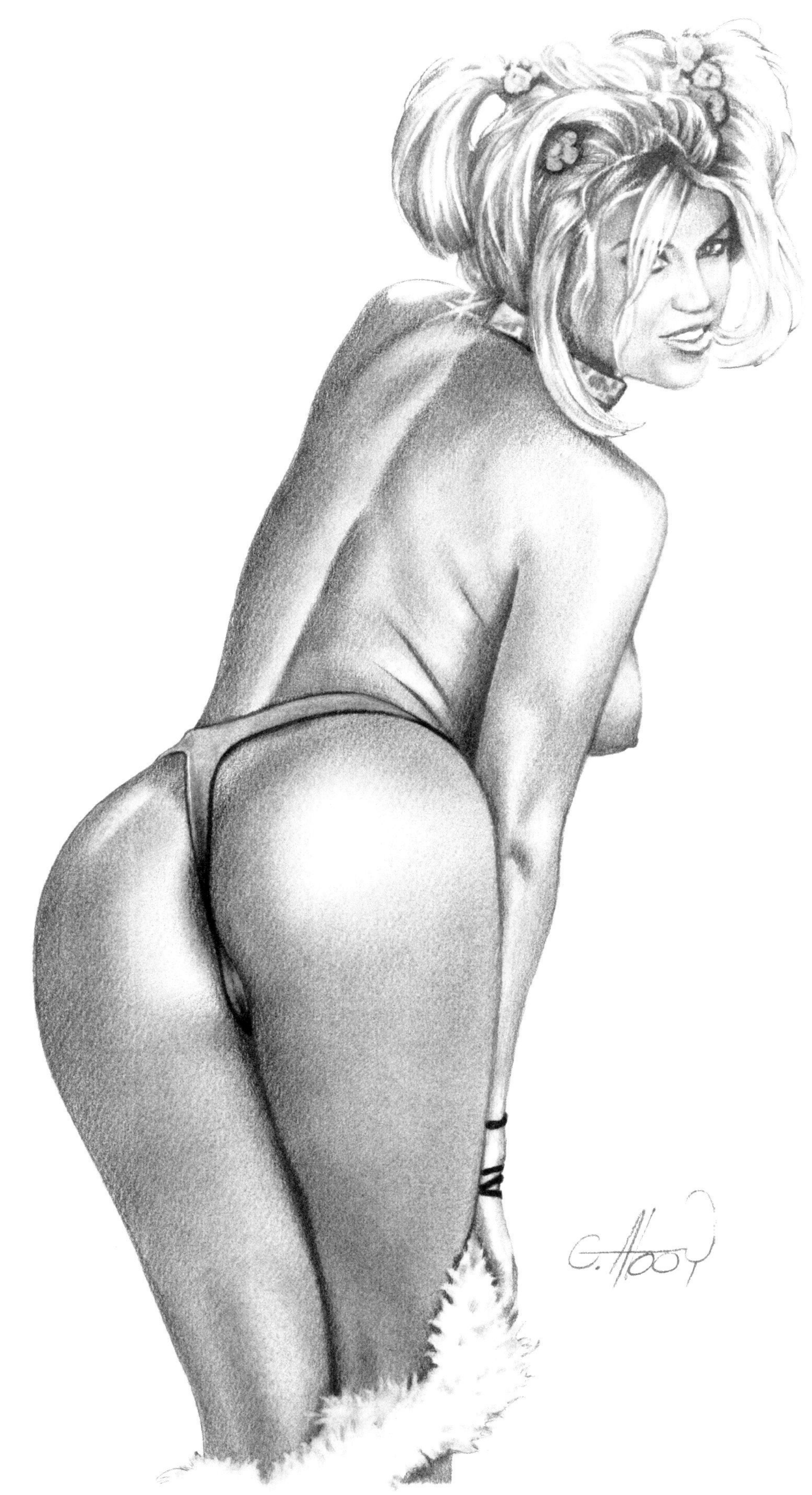

Suzette

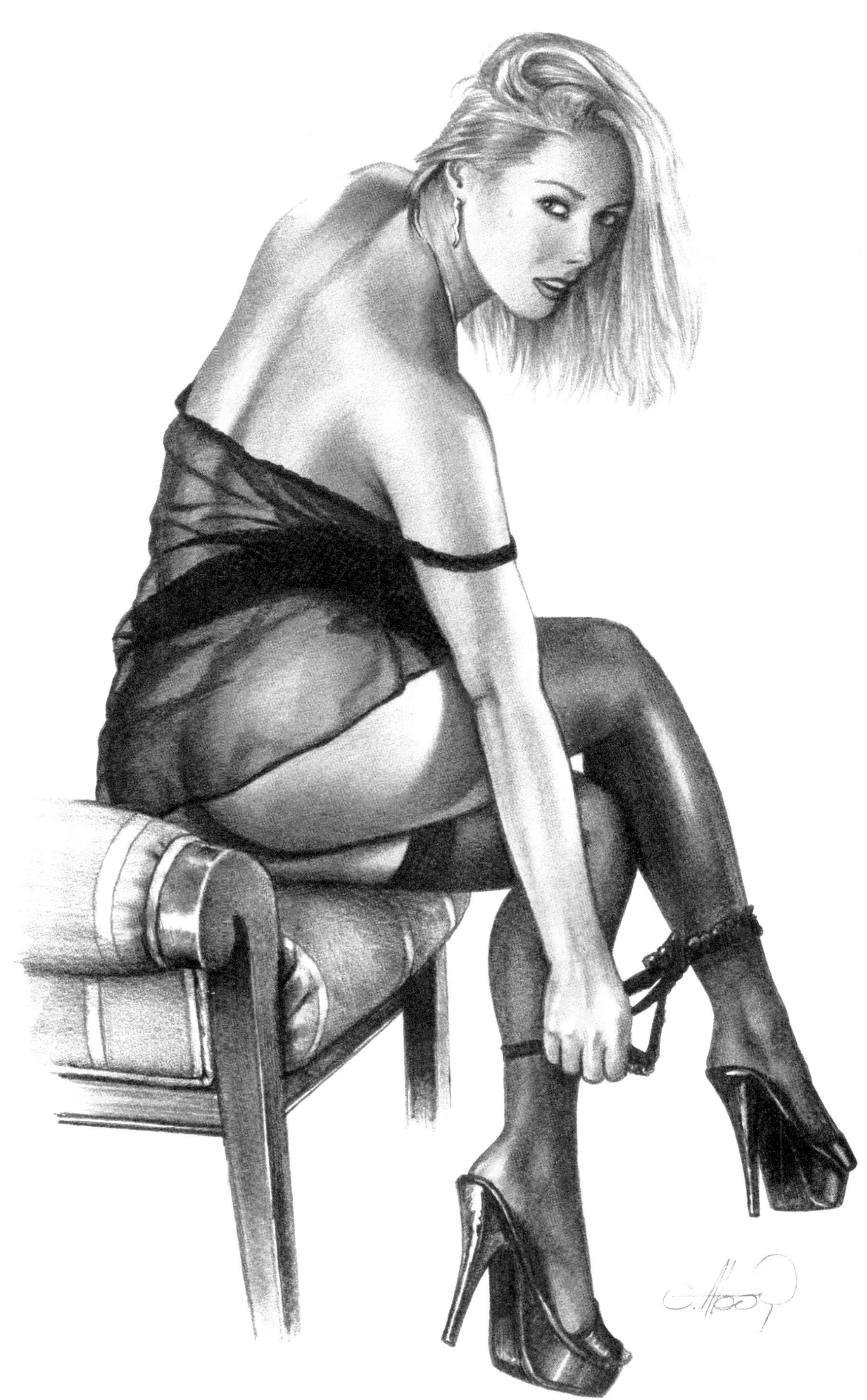

The Night is Young

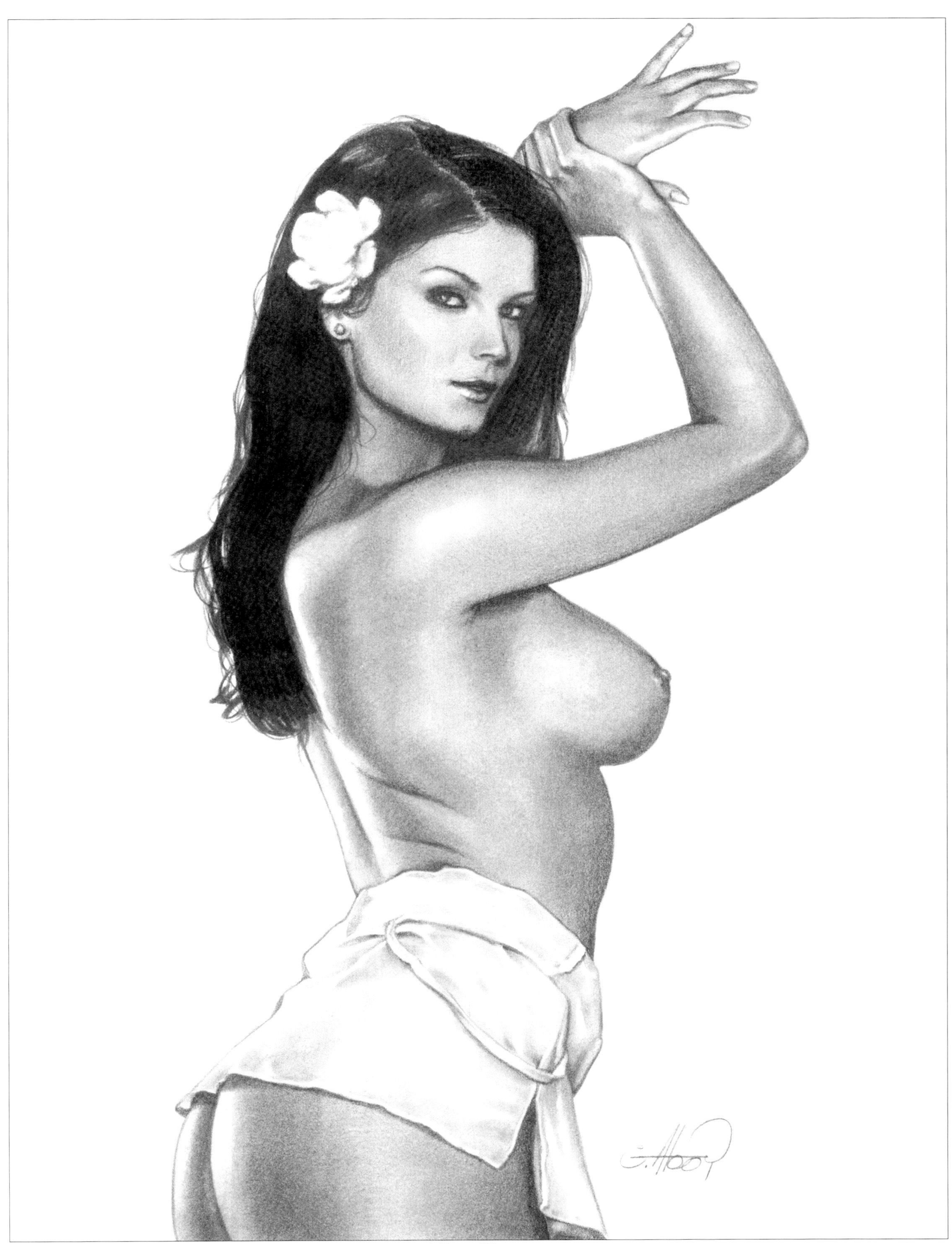

A Rare Flower

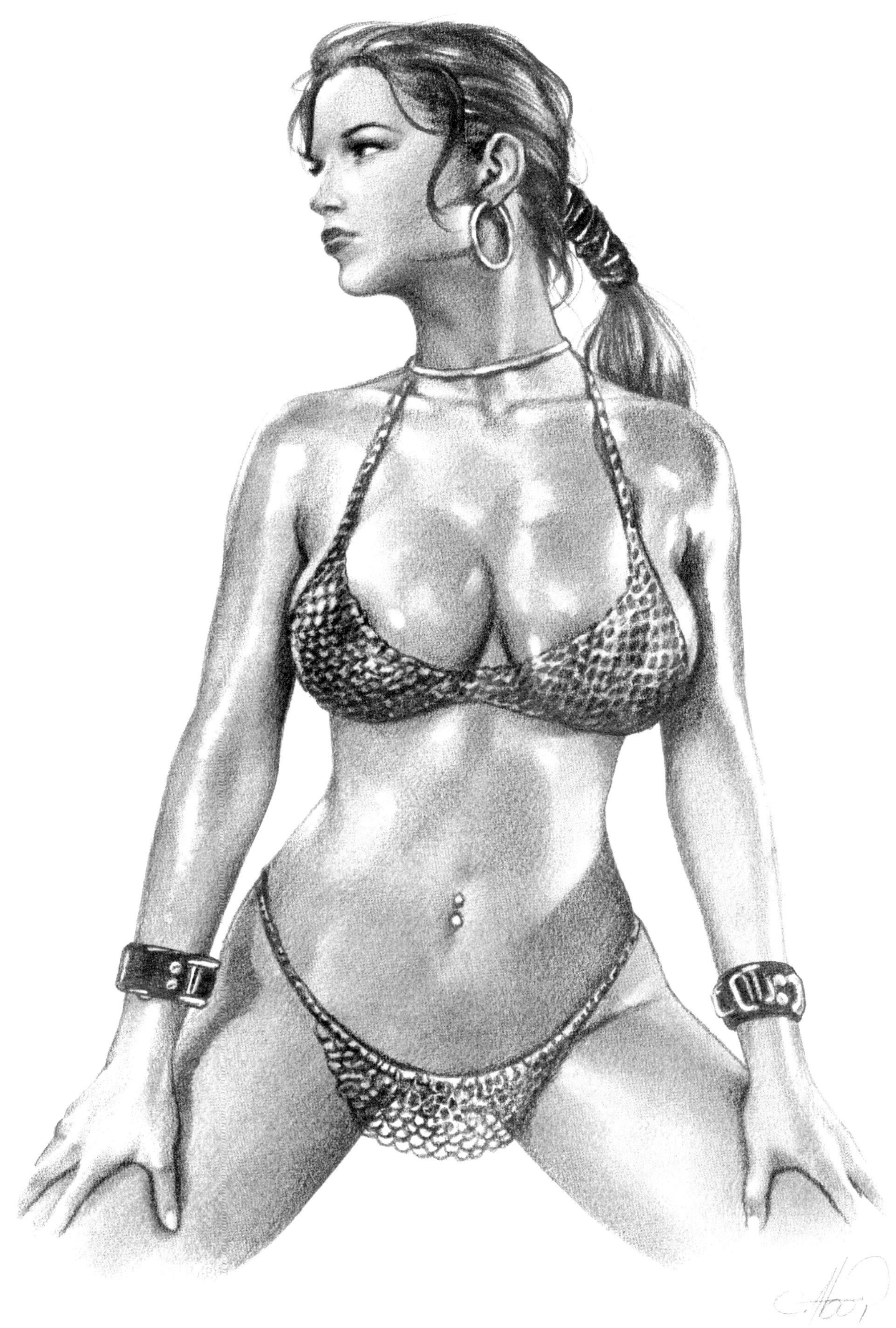

Heat

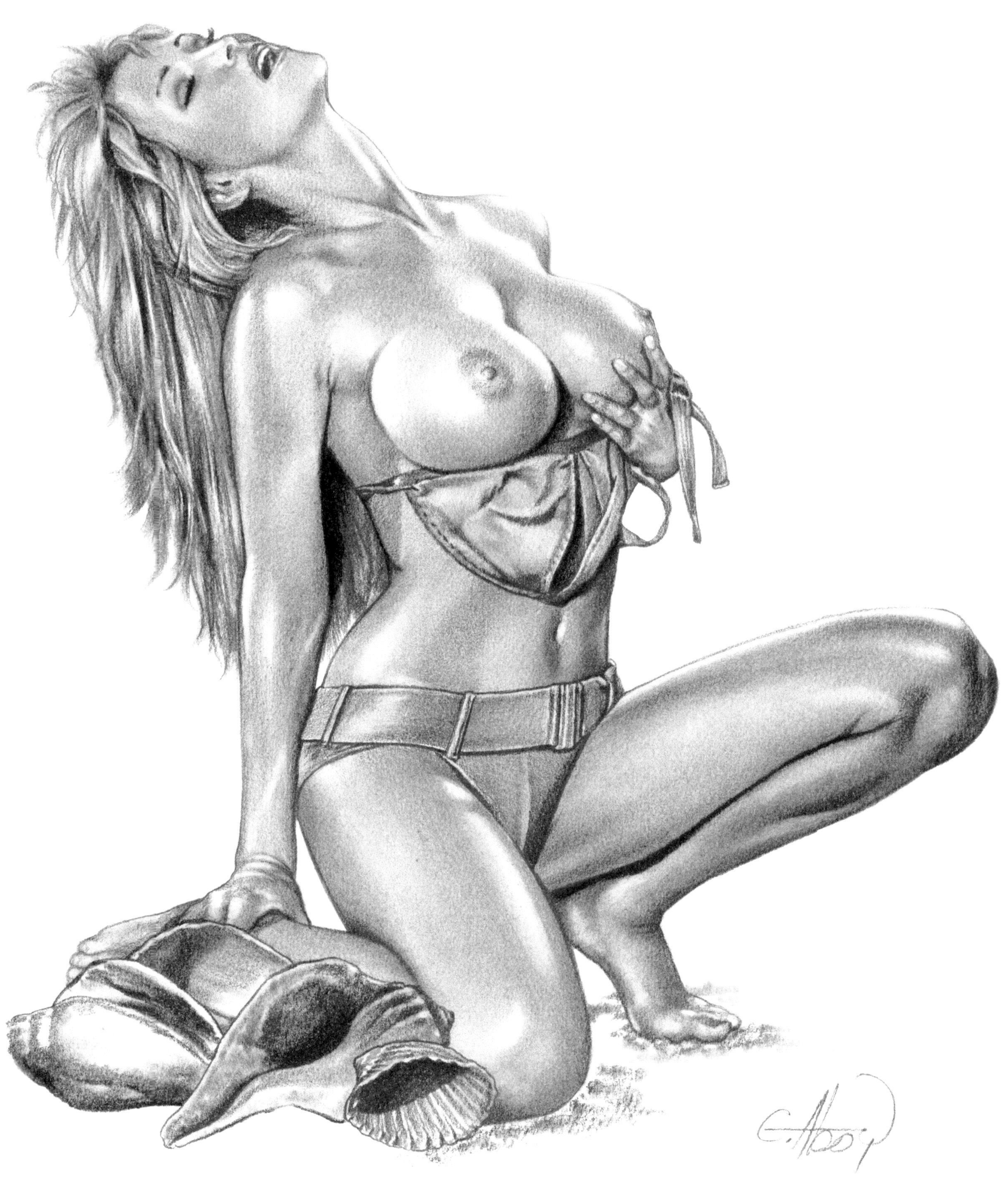

Nice Shells

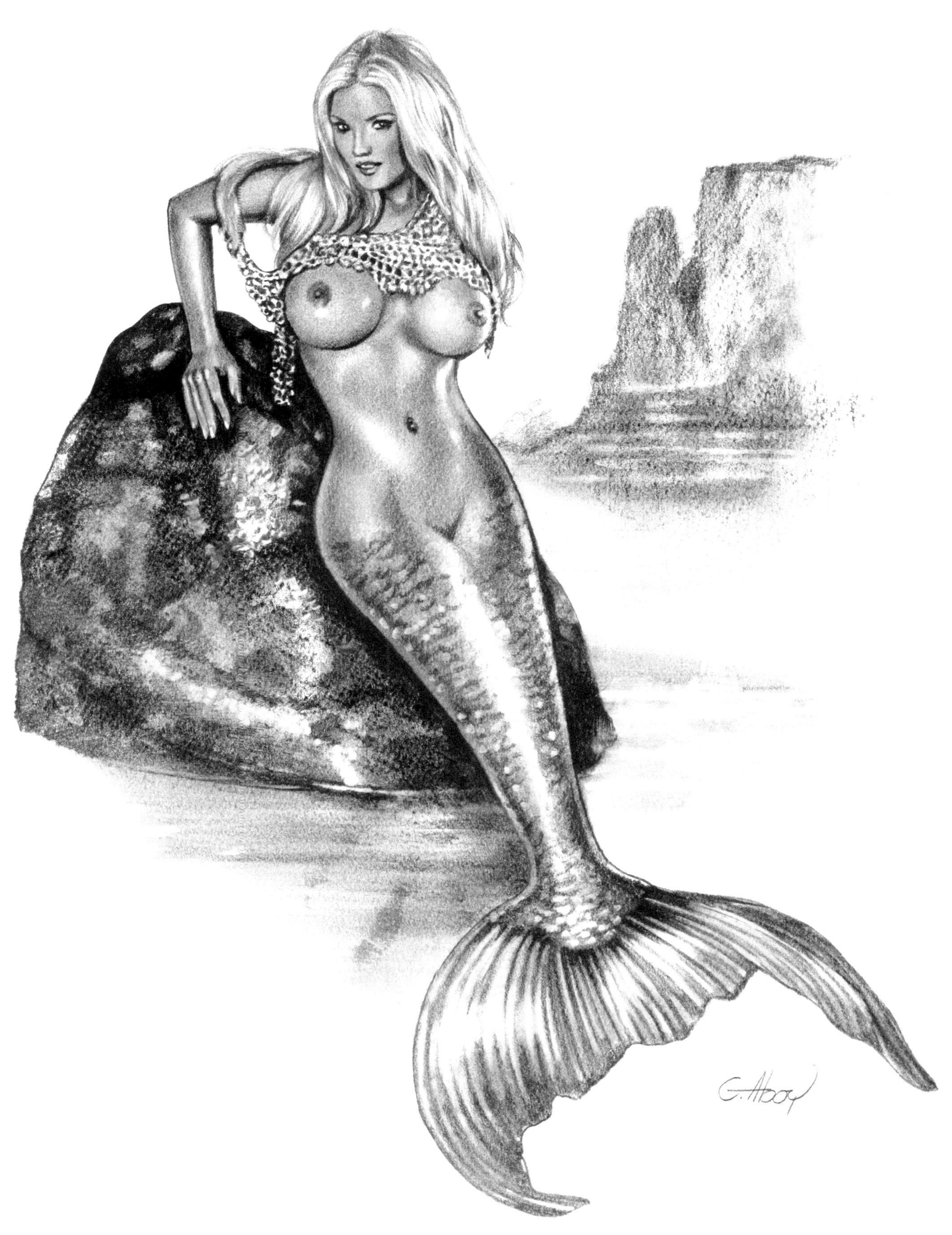

The Ocean's Bounty

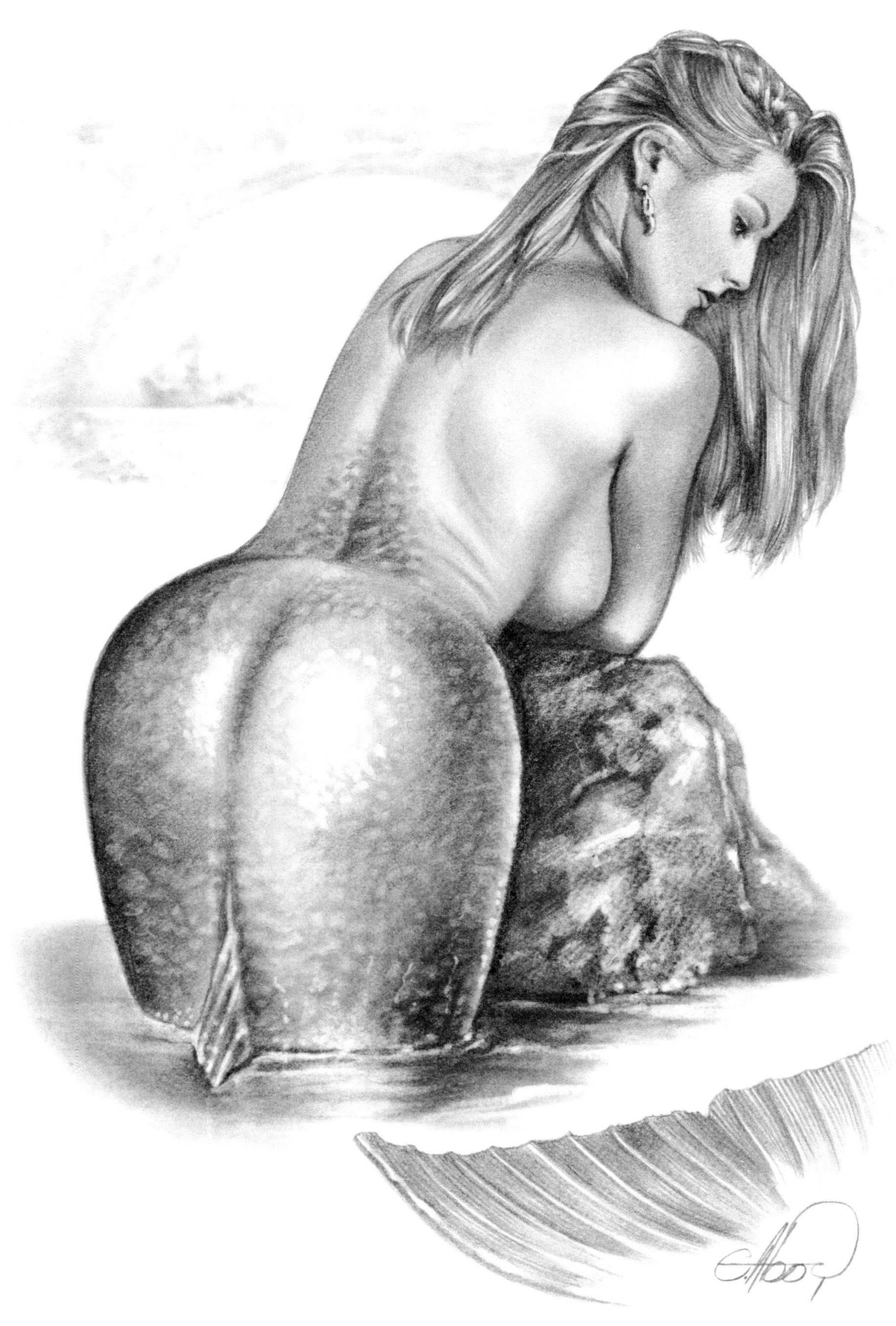

Sail Away

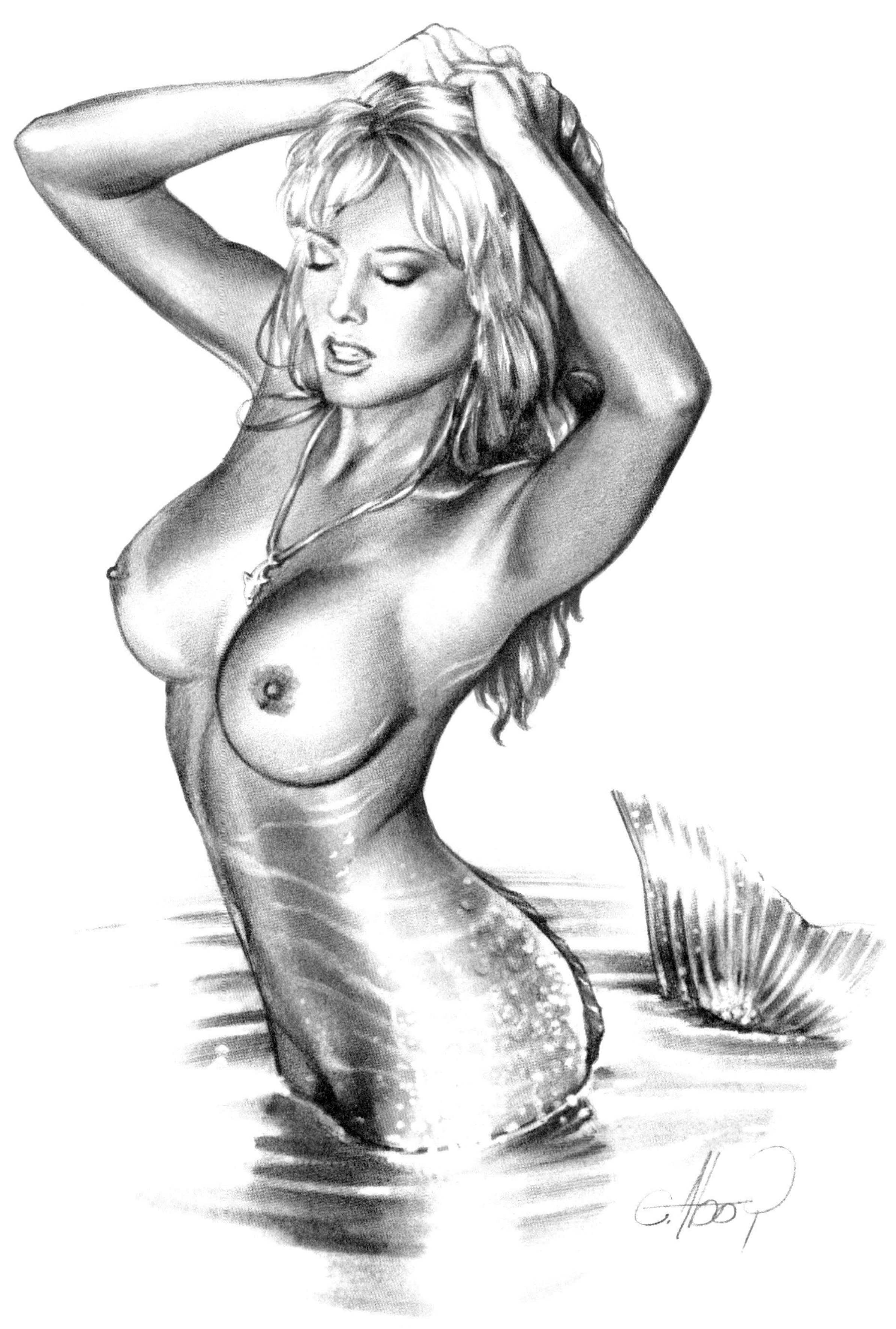

Siren's Lament

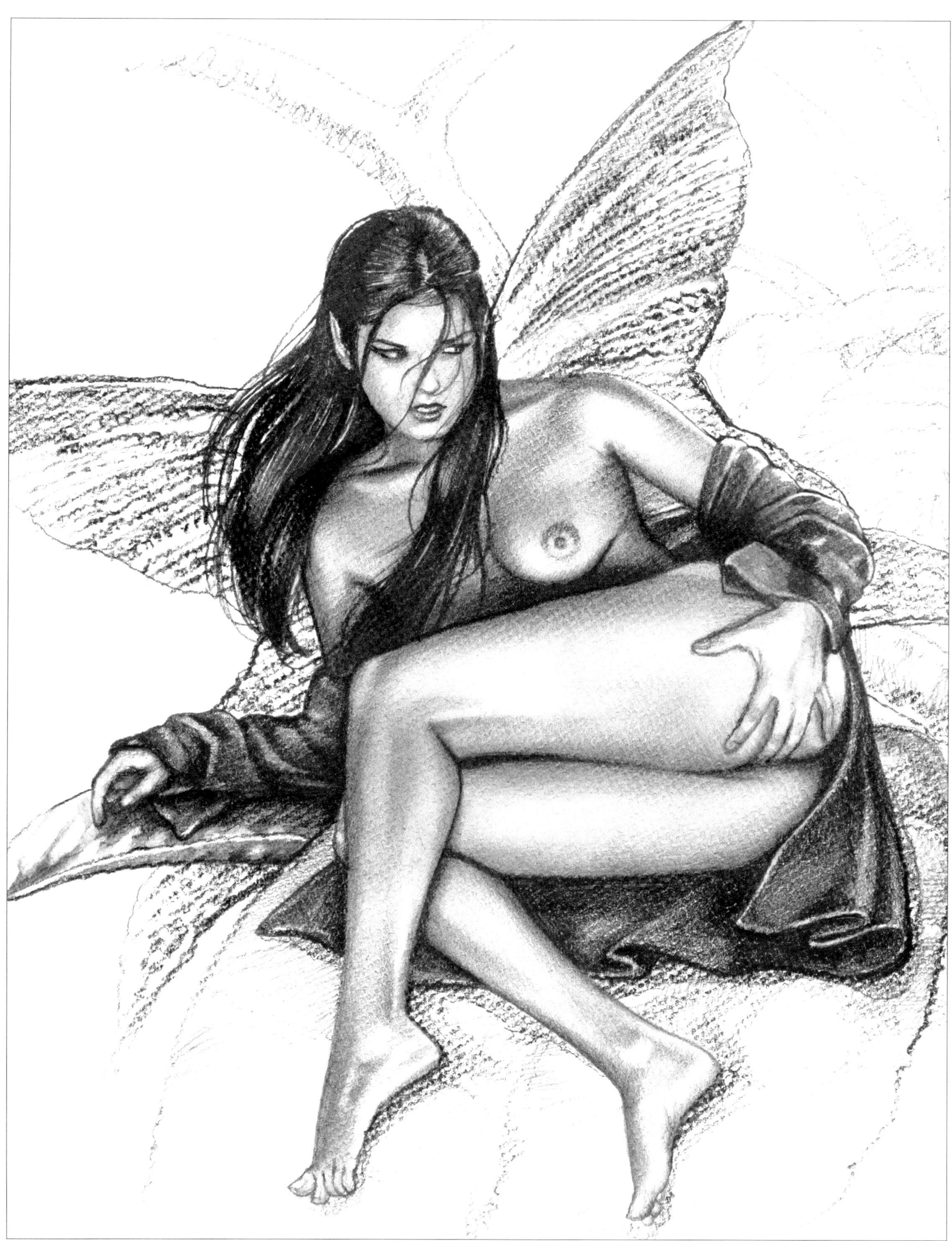

A Fairy's Intuition

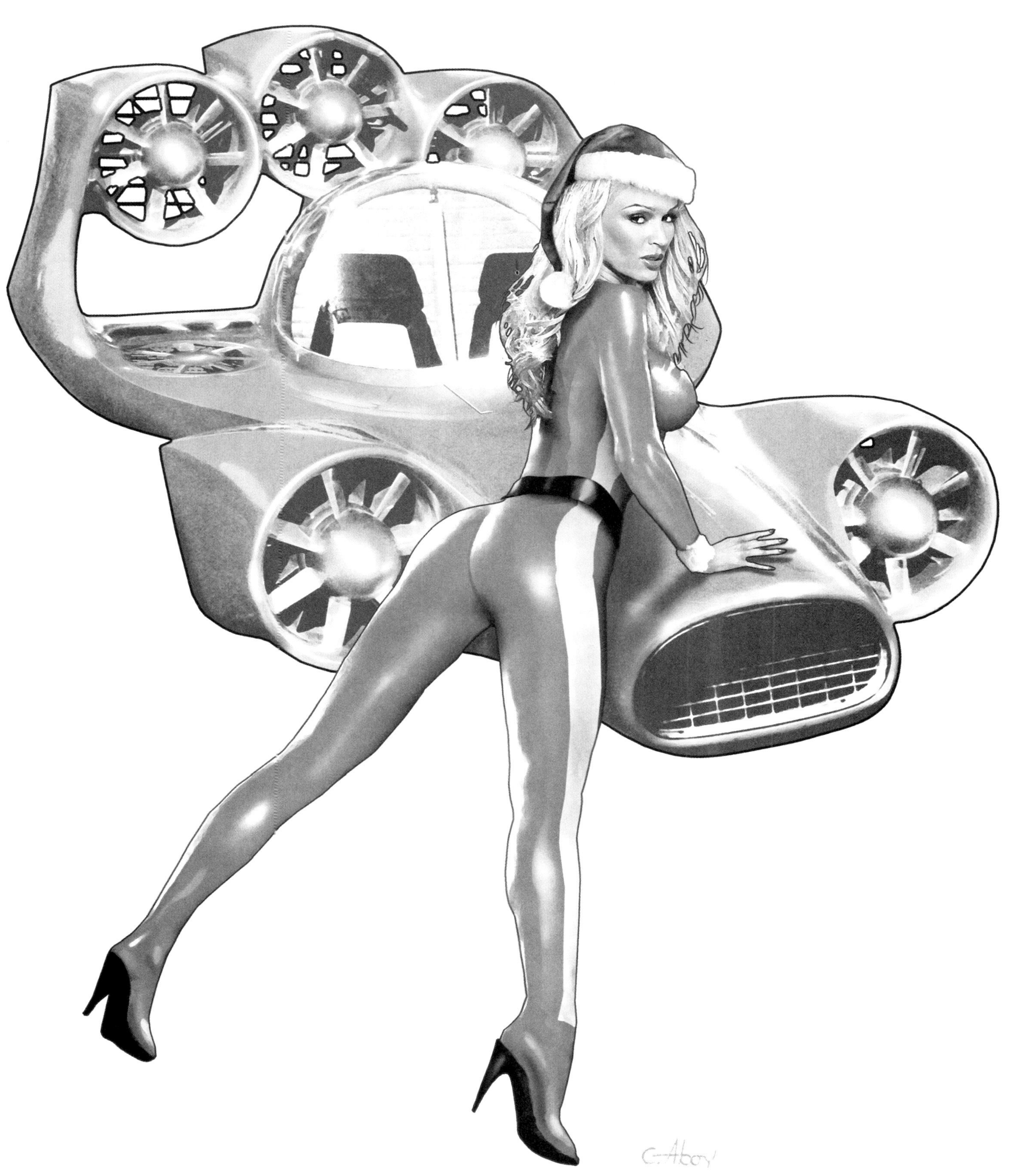

Santa's New Whip

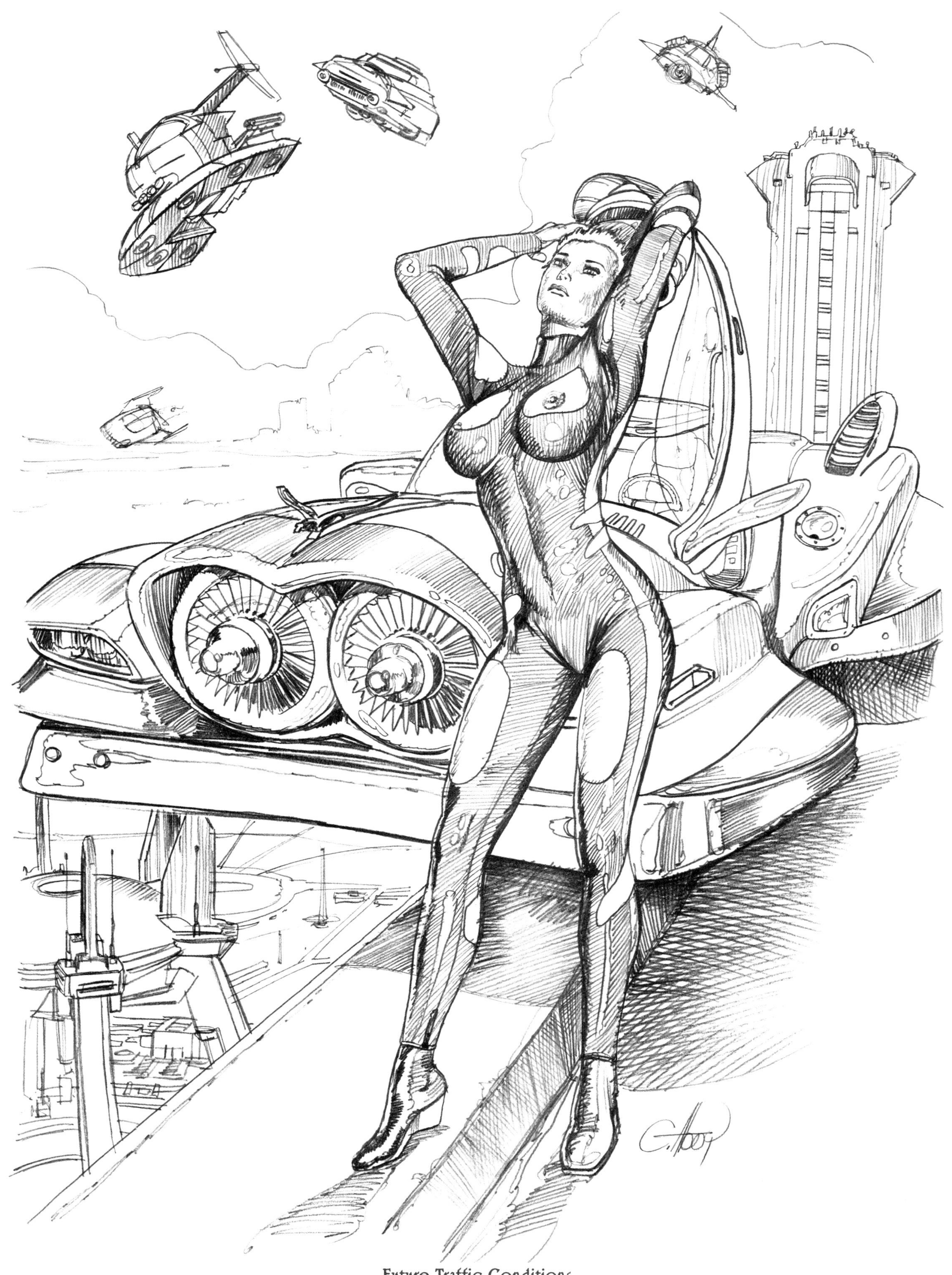

Future Traffic Conditions

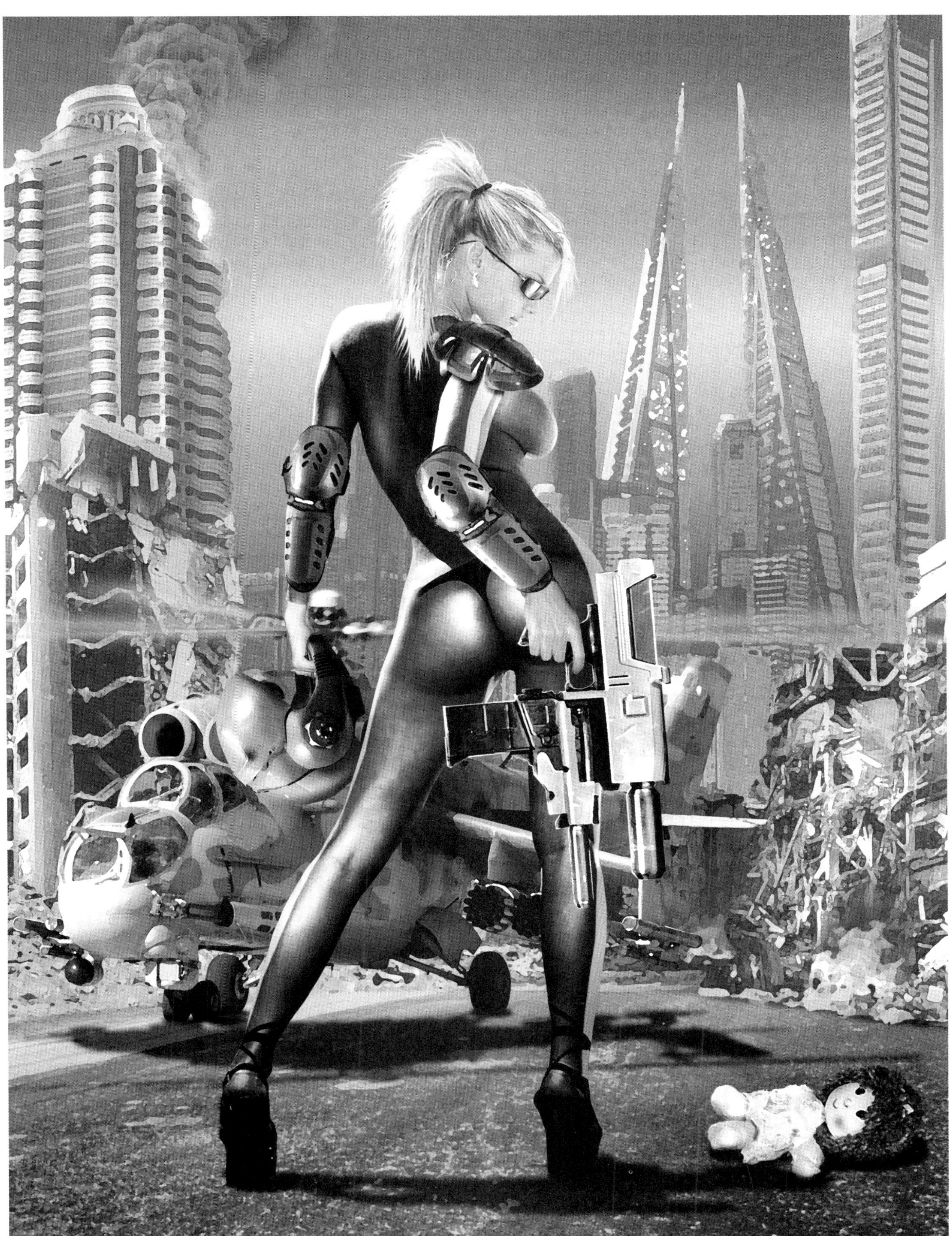

Toys Are For Breaking

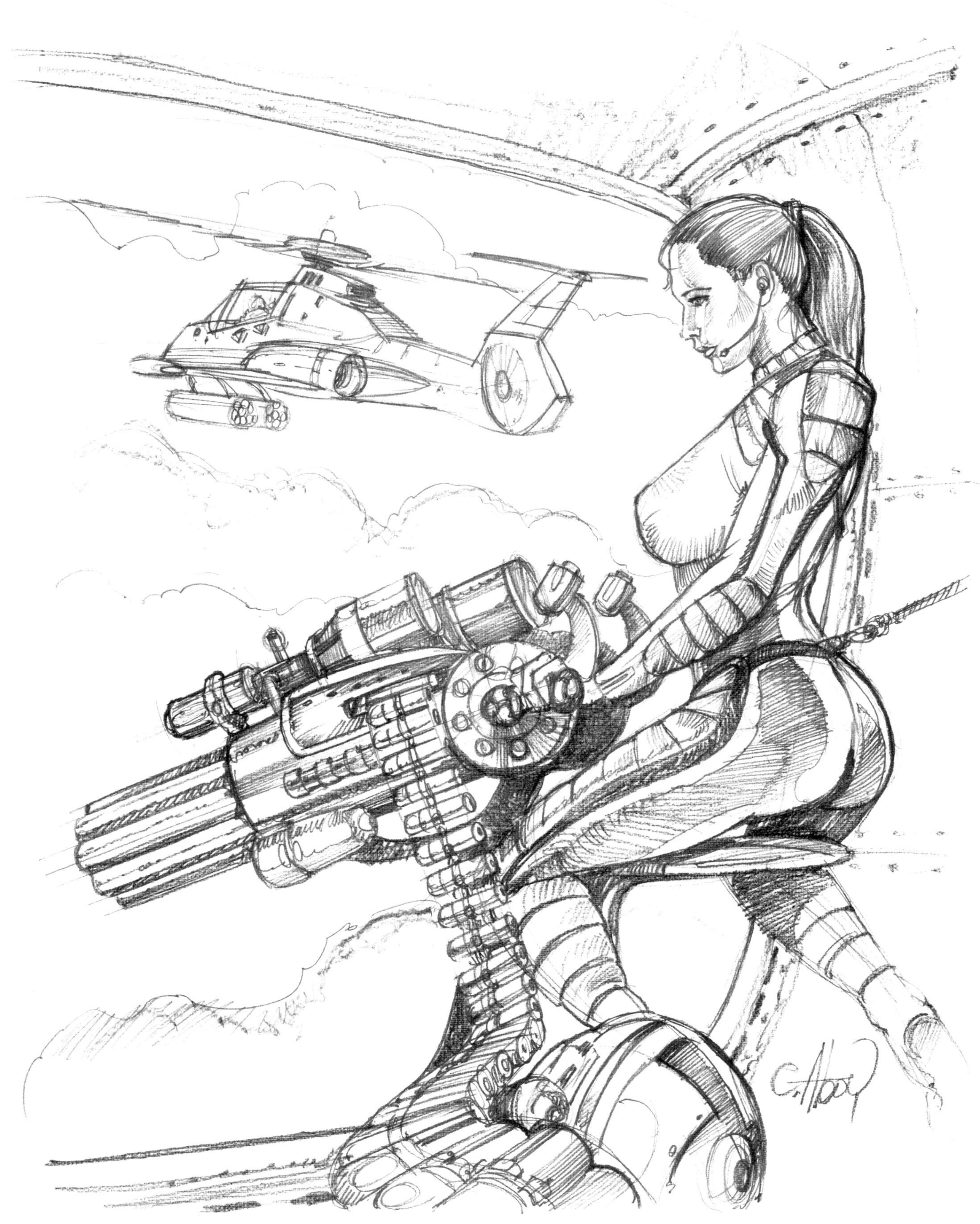

Tail Gunner

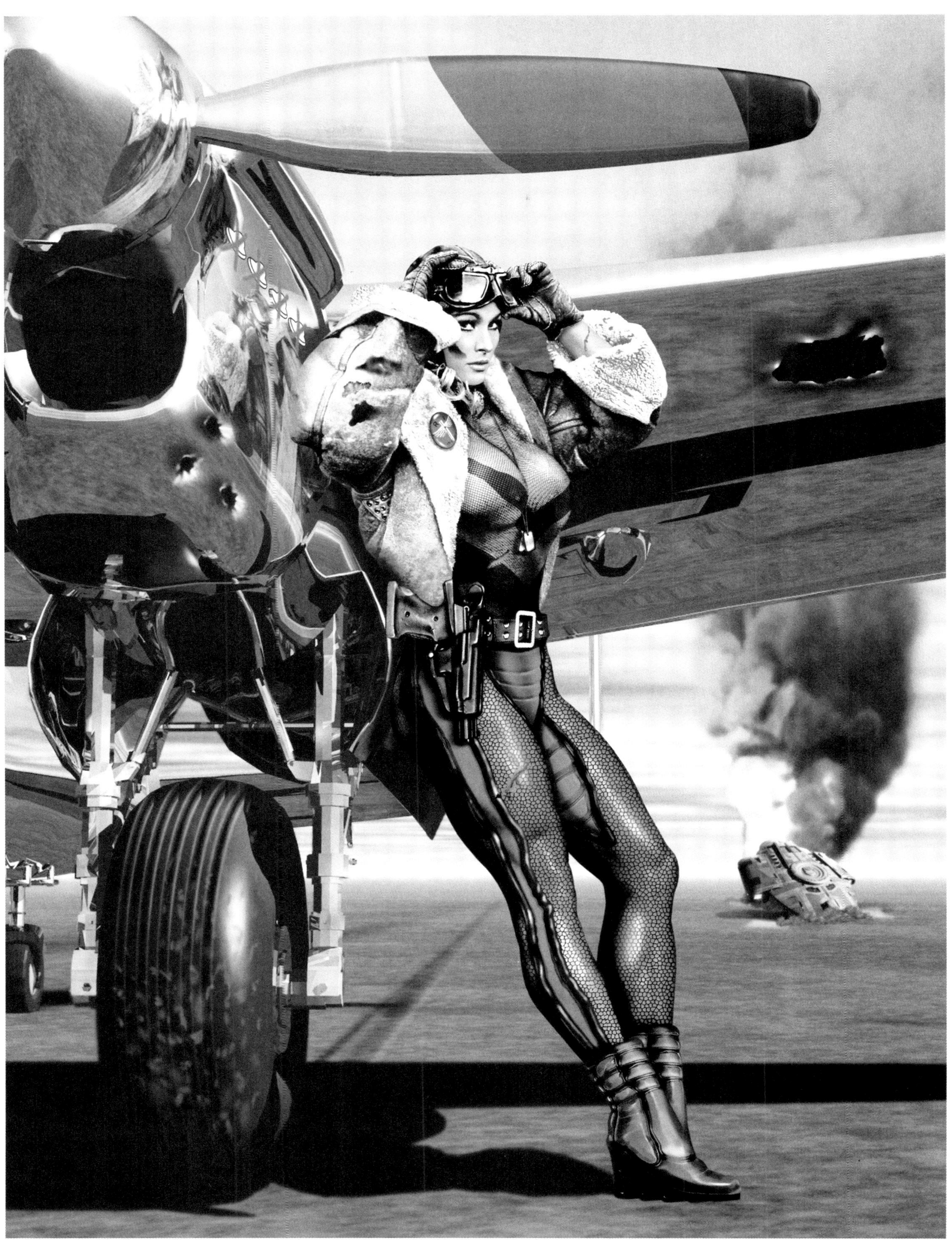

Old School Take Down!

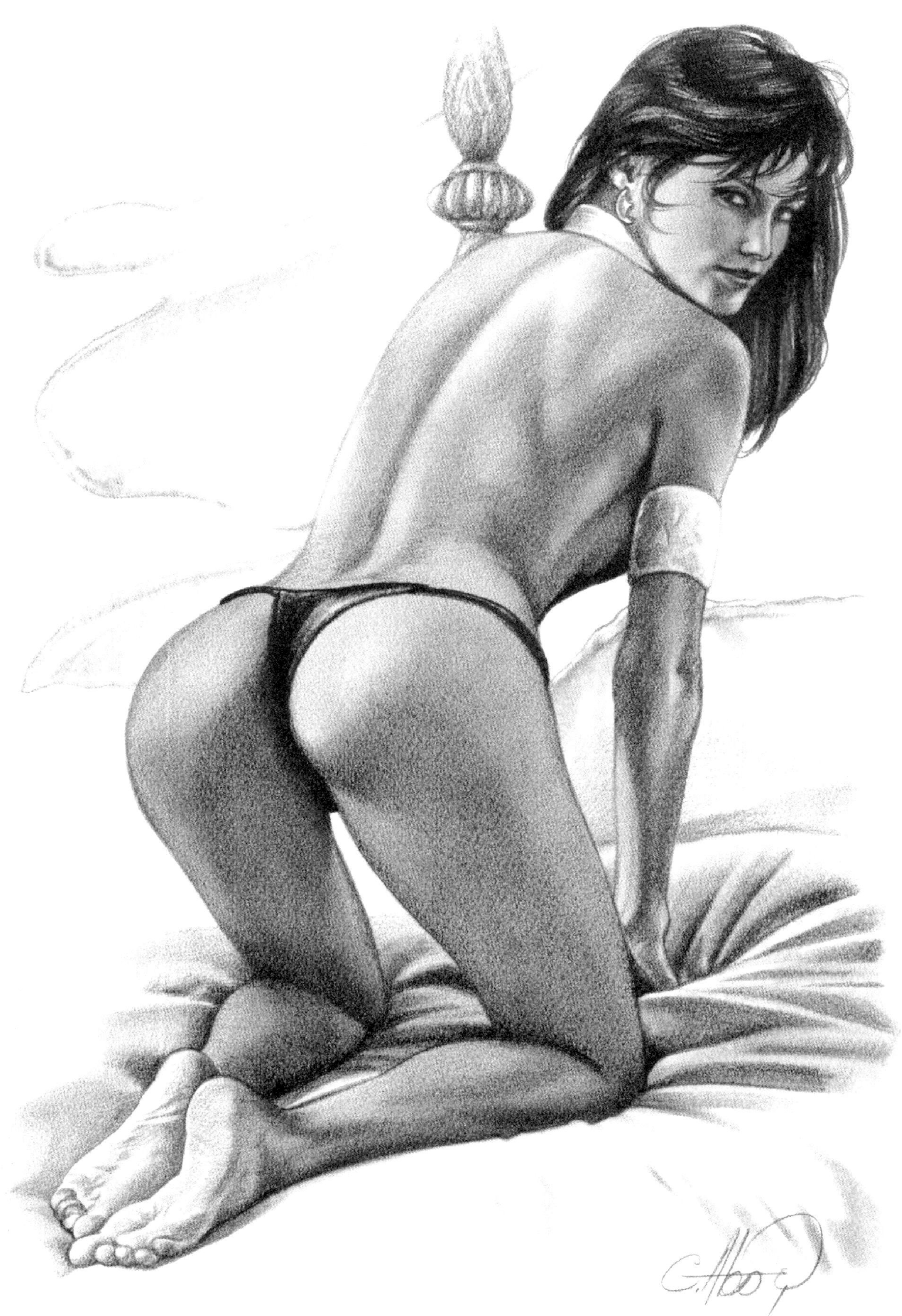

Happy Ending